Teacher's Resource Guide

Saddleback
Lifeskills

Moving Out on Your Own

Everyday Household Tasks

Health and Safety

Managing Money

Consumer Spending

Job Search

Getting Ahead at Work

Community Resources

Public Transportation and Travel

Car and Driver

Development and Production: Laurel Associates, Inc.
Cover Design: Black Eagle Productions

SADDLEBACK
PUBLISHING·INC.
Three Watson
Irvine, CA 92618-2767
Website: www.sdlback.com

ISBN 1-56254-574-4

Printed in the United States of America
10 09 08 07 06   9 8 7 6 5 4 3 2 1

CONTENTS

THE WORKTEXTS: The 10 worktexts in the *Saddleback Lifeskills Series* will provide students a thorough introduction to the "must have" competencies, concepts, and vocabulary they need to achieve independence in the adult world. The compact, two-page lessons—32 in each worktext—are each tightly focused on a particular subtopic to guarantee comprehension and build a foundation for further practice and skill development. The back-of-the-book list of key words in each text may be used at the teacher's discretion for both preview and review of essential vocabulary.

In all, the 320 lessons in the program provide a world of crucial lifeskills information to middle-school through adult students. The high-utility topics run the gamut from personal grooming to shopping for groceries, reading a map, following directions, preparing for a job interview, applying for a driver's license, buying a bus pass, reading prescription labels, operating jumper cables, and so on.

THE TEACHER'S RESOURCE GUIDE: A total of 60 reproducible exercises, six per worktext, are included to support and extend the primary instruction. Besides reinforcing the topic-related instruction, these ancillary worksheets are designed to strengthen critical language-arts skills.

Complete answer keys for both the worktext lessons and the reproducibles are also provided in this guide.

TEACHING TIPS: Your students—like all of us—are most interested in things that relate to themselves. That's why it's always effective to *personalize* the subject matter whenever possible.

• Before assigning a lesson, "warm up" your students by eliciting their opinions or experiences with the general topic. Before a lesson on *emergency health care*, for example, ask volunteers to share an experience they might have had in a hospital emergency room. Before a lesson on *job-hunting*, ask a few students for their opinions of the "best" and "worst" jobs. Have them explain their reasoning. Before a lesson on *consumer spending*, invite students to offer examples of the exaggerated claims used in advertising.

• Notice that the question page in each lesson contains a simple math application of the concept presented. It's easy to extend these small exercises when you're going over the answers with your class. Ask a student who answered correctly to demonstrate his or her calculations on the chalkboard while explaining his or her reasoning.

• Challenge students to use topic-related vocabulary in classroom discussions following a lesson. Offer recognition of some kind, e.g., his or her name under the heading *Today's Word Wizard* on the chalkboard, to the student who correctly uses the most new words in context.

• Extend the "On Your Own" exercise at the end of each question page in the form of a short writing assignment, either for homework or "extra credit." Examples: Write a "Work Wanted" ad for a job you would like to have. Describe your idea of a "perfect apartment." Make a "question guide" to help obtain information about membership at a local health club.

—BOOK 1—
MOVING OUT ON YOUR OWN

UNIT 1: READINESS FOR INDEPENDENCE

Lesson 1: Knowledge and Skills Checklist

THINKING IT OVER: Numbers 1, 2, 4, 5, 7, and 8 should be checked.

SYNONYMS AND ANTONYMS: 1. readiness   2. wise   3. S   4. A   5. S   6. A   7. A

EVERYDAY MATH: 1. low   2. 30

GIVING EXAMPLES: Sample answers:
1. administered first aid to a child who skinned her knee   2. decided not to smoke   3. scrambled eggs; hamburgers; grilled cheese sandwich   4. suit and tie

ON YOUR OWN: Sample answer: parallel park a car

Lesson 2: Attitudes Assessment

THINKING IT OVER: 1. P   2. N   3. N   4. N   5. P   6. P

SYNONYMS: 1. d   2. e   3. f   4. c   5. b   6. a

INFERENCE: 1. eye color   2. moody

KEY VOCABULARY: 1. criticism   2. insecure   3. compromise   4. attitude   5. immature   6. tardy

ON YOUR OWN: Answers will vary.

Lesson 3: Budgeting Time

THINKING IT OVER: 1. yes   2. no   3. yes   4. yes   5. no

EVERYDAY MATH: 1. 80 hours   2. 11 hours

KEY VOCABULARY: 1. busy   2. scheduled   3. routine   4. method   5. keep in

CAUSE AND EFFECT: 1. so you won't forget them   2. it helps you focus your efforts on what you have to get done that day

ON YOUR OWN: Answers will vary.

Lesson 4: Budgeting Money

THINKING IT OVER: 1. T   2. F   3. T   4. F

EVERYDAY MATH: 1. 8%   2. $264.50   3. $793.50

KEY VOCABULARY: 1. a plan for spending money   2. the amount of money you have coming in   3. pay for it without undue sacrifice   4. change it   5. add to it   6. lessen it

EXTEND THE LESSON: Sample answers: reduce food bill to 10%; reduce clothing bill to 5%; reduce entertainment to 5%

ON YOUR OWN: Sample answers: savings, tuition, life insurance, gardening supplies, hobbies

Unit 1: Review

A. Sample answers: 1. ability to work hard; ability to cook simple dishes   2. "I'm always right" causes me to resent constructive criticism.   3. write appointments on a calendar and make a to-do list   4. make a budget

B. 1. attitudes   2. calendar   3. budget

C. Answers will vary.

UNIT 2: FINDING AN APARTMENT

Lesson 1: A Housing Checklist

THINKING IT OVER: 1. c   2. b   3. b   4. a   5. c

EVERYDAY MATH: $400

KEY VOCABULARY: 1. pros and cons   2. vacancy   3. Brainstorming   4. budget

INFORMAL LANGUAGE: pinching pennies

ON YOUR OWN: Answers will vary.

Lesson 2: Comparing Classified Rental Ads

THINKING IT OVER: 1. F   2. F   3. F   4. F   5. T   6. T

ABBREVIATIONS: 1. d   2. f   3. e   4. b   5. a   6. c

EVERYDAY MATH: 1. $1,400   2. $675

SEQUENCING: 2, 4, 6, 3, 1, 5

KEY VOCABULARY: 1. sublease   2. first, last   3. studio   4. security deposit

ON YOUR OWN: Answers will vary.

Lesson 3: Rental Application

THINKING IT OVER: 1. date you plan to move in   2. so the new landlord can check if you pay rent on time   3. so the new landlord can know if you were kicked out for any reason   4. to know where to reach you during business hours, if necessary   5. to determine if you can afford to pay rent   6. so the landlord can determine if you're reliable   7. in case it's parked illegally, he or she can ask you to move it before it gets towed

EVERYDAY MATH: 1. $1,935   2. $483.75 to $580.50

KEY VOCABULARY: 1. lives there   2. had before 3. pays someone to do a job   4. sudden situation that needs immediate attention 5. can   6. prove it is true

DRAWING CONCLUSIONS: to protect you in case the landlord tries to keep the deposit illegally

ON YOUR OWN: Answers will vary.

Lesson 4: Rules for Roommates

THINKING IT OVER: 1. F   2. T   3. T   4. F   5. F

KEY VOCABULARY: 1. make it more attractive 2. minor   3. go bad over time   4. money 5. without any special effort   6. common

EVERYDAY MATH: 1. $875   2. 8½   3. $485

CAUSE AND EFFECT: There would be friction between the roommates, which would have to be resolved.

ON YOUR OWN: Answers will vary.

Unit 2: Review

A. 1. Sample answer: number of bedrooms and cost   2. A condo is owned by an individual; in a 10-unit building, there might be 10 different owners. An apartment is a multi-unit building owned by one person or one company.   3. to determine if you can afford the rent   4. You can split the bills and you can have instant company.

B. 1. efficiency apartment   2. security deposit   3. stove, refrigerator

C. Answers will vary.

D. Sample answer: Tell the roommate the friend will have to pay to cover the difference.

UNIT 3: MOVING IN AND GETTING SETTLED

Lesson 1: Change of Address Cards

THINKING IT OVER: 1. Puerto Rico residents 2. must fill out a separate form   3. must fill out a separate form   4. Business   5. three

SYNONYMS AND ANTONYMS: 1. A   2. S   3. S   4. A 5. S   6. individual   7. temporary

EVERYDAY MATH: 42; 6

DRAWING CONCLUSIONS: The post office forwarded it to her new address.

ON YOUR OWN: Answers will vary.

Lesson 2: Ordering Telephone and Utilities Services

THINKING IT OVER: 1. He wrapped breakable objects in paper; he asked friends to help in the move. 2. Call the local phone company for a new number; call the long-distance company to ensure uninterrupted service; have gas, electric, and water service connected.

INFERENCE: 1. so they'll have time to test lines, if necessary   2. No. If you waited until the day of the move, the services might get turned on too late in the day.   3. No. If they were turned off the same day, you might not have electricity when you wanted to do a final vacuuming.

KEY VOCABULARY: 1. ensure   2. arrange 3. details   4. uninterrupted   5. grateful 6. reminder   7. siblings

ON YOUR OWN: Answers will vary.

Lesson 3: Buying Essential Household Goods

THINKING IT OVER: 1. T   2. T   3. F   4. T   5. F

EVERYDAY MATH: 1. $1,440   2. $425

KEY VOCABULARY: 1. needed   2. getting 3. easier   4. is   5. year

MAKING INFERENCES: 1. b   2. a   3. c

ON YOUR OWN: Answers will vary.

Lesson 4: Renting a Moving Truck

THINKING IT OVER: 1. trailer   2. 17-foot van 3. strong enough   4. weeks

EVERYDAY MATH: $122.40

KEY VOCABULARY: 1. pay them to help you 2. choices   3. do not   4. 18 or 21 5. is recognized by the law

GIVING ADVICE: Sample answer: Force yourself to whittle down your belongings. It's not worth the money it would cost to move everything.

ON YOUR OWN: Answers will vary.

Unit 3: Review

A. 1. Sample answers: bank, school 2. Turn off old ones the day after the move; turn on new ones the day before the move, to ensure uninterrupted service.   3. shop at discount stores; read classified newspaper ads; make them yourself   4. fee for rental, mileage, gas, insurance, deposit

B. 1. electricity   2. telephone   3. Sample answers: bed, table, chairs

C. Answers will vary.

D. Sell it and use the money to buy another used one; or buy a slipcover and hide the couch that way.

UNIT 4: SOLVING COMMON PROBLEMS

Lesson 1: Dos and Don'ts for Tenants

Crossed out phrases on page 36 should be: He will train the vines to grow around the deck railing, etc.; He'll put some speakers outside on the deck, too; This way he can carry all of his laundry to the laundry room at once, etc.; dry towels outside; and store it on the deck; Paint the bedroom walls red

THINKING IT OVER: 1. b   2. a   3. c   4. b   5. a

EVERYDAY MATH: June 26

KEY VOCABULARY: 1. A   2. A   3. S   4. S   5. A

MAKING INFERENCES: 1. The plants might fall and hurt someone.   2. The next tenant might not like it, and it's too hard and expensive to redecorate between tenants.

ON YOUR OWN: Answers will vary.

Lesson 2: Unexpected Expenses–Revising Your Budget

Circled expenses on page 38 should be: Utilities, Phone, Savings, Charities, Charge Accounts, Medical/dental, Household maintenance, Food, Personal maintenance, and Recreation

THINKING IT OVER: 1. F   2. T   3. T   4. F   5. T   6. T

SUMMARIZING: Figure out how to pay it. Revise the budget to avoid going into debt.

EVERYDAY MATH: 1. $133.75   2. 6 months

KEY VOCABULARY: 1. h   2. g   3. d   4. i   5. f   6. e   7. b   8. a   9. c

ON YOUR OWN: Answers will vary.

Lesson 3: Revising Rules for Roommates

THINKING IT OVER: 1. a   2. c   3. b   4. c

EVERYDAY MATH: 1. $25 a week   2. $975

KEY VOCABULARY 1. asked   2. save   3. no   4. seeing   5. old

IDIOMS 1. contributes   2. refrigerator   3. right

ON YOUR OWN: Answers will vary.

Lesson 4: Tenants' Legal Rights

THINKING IT OVER: 1. T   2. F   3. T   4. F   5. T

EVERYDAY MATH: $425; Discuss the problem with the landlord.

KEY VOCABULARY: 1. trivial   2. take it away   3. permitted   4. rent   5. live there   6. enough

CAUSE AND EFFECT: Tenants might get a mold problem, which is a health hazard. Also, damage to ceiling, carpeting, and furniture might result.

ON YOUR OWN: I'd repair it myself and deduct the cost from the rent.

Unit 4: Review

A. 1. Sample answers: making loud noise; cluttering up common areas with trash or possessions   2. revise your budget   3. speak to the roommate; if nothing changes, they should ask the roommate to leave and then find another, more responsible person   4. (See page 42)

B. 1. playing the TV too loudly   2. unexpected expense; dental work, car repair, etc.   3. Answers will vary.

C. 1. Answers will vary.   2. If the tenant pays a damage deposit, it will be okay.

—BOOK 2—
EVERYDAY HOUSEHOLD TASKS

UNIT 1: GROCERY SHOPPING

Lesson 1: Grocery Staples

THINKING IT OVER: 1. b   2. c   3. a   4. b

EVERYDAY MATH: 1 more serving

KEY VOCABULARY: 1. a food item you use again and again   2. a cabinet, closet, or small room used for food storage   3. eating the appropriate number of servings from the six food groups as recommended by the USDA   4. bread, cereal, rice, and pasta   5. milk, yogurt, and cheese

ON YOUR OWN: Answers will vary.

Lesson 2: Reading Grocery Ads

THINKING IT OVER: 1. b   2. c   3. a   4. c

EVERYDAY MATH: 1. 79¢ per can because at 3 cans for $3 you would pay $1 per can 2. 2 boxes at $2.25 each because that's $4.50 total, 19¢ less than the other deal

KEY VOCABULARY: 1. acquiring something at a price that is advantageous to the buyer 2. you can get only 3 at the special price 3. a product a store sells at a loss in order to attract more customers 4. review prices at different stores, or determine which brand or size of product is more economical based on lowest unit price (e.g., "per ounce" price)

ON YOUR OWN: Answers will vary.

Lesson 3: Meal Planning

THINKING IT OVER: 1. a 2. c 3. c 4. a

EVERYDAY MATH: 1. 1 serving 2. 4 servings

KEY VOCABULARY: 1. bread, cereal, rice, pasta 2. advice that something be done 3. before it is due or needed 4. an assortment, a number of different things

ON YOUR OWN: Answers will vary.

Lesson 4: Getting the Best Value

THINKING IT OVER: 1. a 2. c 3. a 4. a

EVERYDAY MATH: 1a. the 28-ounce can 1b. 2¢ 2. $2.04

KEY VOCABULARY: 1. a helpful hint 2. inspect casually at a leisurely pace 3. items that are combined to create a new and different item 4. the cost per ounce or other measurable unit

ON YOUR OWN: Answers will vary.

Unit 1: Review

A. 1. salt, pepper, flour, catsup, spices 2. A "loss leader" is an item sold at a loss in order to attract customers. A "special" is a temporary offer that benefits the customer but still makes a profit for the seller. 3. 2 to 3 ounces meat, poultry, or fish; 1 to $1\frac{1}{2}$ cups cooked dried beans; 2 to 3 eggs; 4 to 6 tablespoons peanut butter; $\frac{2}{3}$ to 1 cup nuts 4. Answers will vary. 5. Answers will vary.

B. 1. seasonal 2. unit price

C. Answers will vary.

UNIT 2: COOKING

Lesson 1: Setting Up a Kitchen

THINKING IT OVER: 1. a 2. c 3. c 4. a

EVERYDAY MATH: $5.94

KEY VOCABULARY: 1. supplies 2. container for storing foods 3. pan 4. pot

EXTENDING THE LESSON: Possible answers: potato masher, omelette pan, ice cream scoop

ON YOUR OWN: Probable answer: Measuring spoons come in standard sizes and give accurate measurements.

Lesson 2: Cookbook

THINKING IT OVER: 1. c 2. a 3. c 4. a

KEY VOCABULARY: 1. chapters in a book listed by page numbers 2. an alphabetized list of items mentioned in a book 3. a mini-dictionary of important words in a book 4. a set of directions on how to cook something

COMPARING: 1. "Vegetables" 2. "Pasta"

EVERYDAY MATH: 1. $2\frac{1}{2}$ cups 2. 6:05

ON YOUR OWN: Answers will vary.

Lesson 3: Time-Savers

THINKING IT OVER: 1. a 2. c 3. a 4. b

EVERYDAY MATH: 1. 8 2. 6:05

KEY VOCABULARY: 1. boil for a short time 2. easy to use

PUTTING DETAILS IN ORDER: 2, 4, 1, 5, 3, 6

ON YOUR OWN: Answers will vary.

Lesson 4: Following Recipe Directions

THINKING IT OVER: 1. a 2. c 3. c 4. a

KEY VOCABULARY: 1. thin, matchlike strips 2. slicing at a 45-degree angle 3. putting the food across a shredding surface to make long, narrow strips

EVERYDAY MATH: 96

RECALLING DETAILS: Probable answer: wash and chop vegetables; heat wok; add a little oil; put vegetables in wok; cook quickly, lifting and turning food constantly

ON YOUR OWN: Answers will vary.

Unit 2: Review

A. Possible answers: 1. mixing bowls, measuring spoons, 10-inch skillet with cover, colander, meat thermometer, 3-quart covered saucepan   2. Table of Contents: to find titles of chapters and where they start. Index: to look up a particular subject. Glossary: to look up a particular word.   3. cooking in bulk; using a food processor   4. Answers will vary.   5. broil, bake, or poach it

B. 1. dry measuring cups   2. on a rack to cool   3. meat thermometer

C. Answers will vary.

UNIT 3: CARING FOR YOUR CLOTHES

Lesson 1: Organizing a Closet and Chest of Drawers

THINKING IT OVER: 1. buttoning top buttons   2. lightly   3. folded   4. far apart

KEY VOCABULARY: 1. b   2. c   3. a   4. b   5. a

EVERYDAY MATH: 24

RECALLING DETAILS: Possible answers:
1. to prevent damage from splinters
2. to discourage pests

ON YOUR OWN: Answers will vary.

Lesson 2: Doing the Laundry

THINKING IT OVER: 1. F   2. T   3. T   4. T   5. F

EVERYDAY MATH: 1. 25   2. 25 cents

KEY VOCABULARY: 1. let it sit in water for a while   2. put water through it to remove soap   3. rub or brush it hard   4. gets smaller

CAUSE AND EFFECT: 1. the whites will pick up some color   2. set the stain

ON YOUR OWN: Answers will vary.

Lesson 3: Information on Clothing Labels

THINKING IT OVER: 1. Read the care label.   2. on the back of the collar or on a side seam   3. shoes, caps, hats, gloves   4. wash with clothing of similar color and brightness

KEY VOCABULARY: 1. how hot or how cold something is   2. a tag sewn in or attached to something   3. directions   4. proper and correct   5. way of doing something   6. laid flat

EVERYDAY MATH: $6.25

DRAWING CONCLUSIONS: They turned pink.

ON YOUR OWN: Possible answers: 1. to make sure an item is washable if you want to avoid dry-cleaning bills; to see if an item has been preshrunk   2. before you wash the item so you use the correct water temperature, wash cycle, and dryer setting

Lesson 4: Ironing, Dry Cleaning, and Storing Clothes

THINKING IT OVER: 1. b   2. c   3. a   4. b

KEY VOCABULARY: 1. slightly wet   2. slight   3. method   4. creased   5. item of clothing   6. dirty

EVERYDAY MATH: 1. $63.20   2. $53.20

SUMMARIZING: Paragraph should reflect information in lesson.

ON YOUR OWN: Answers will vary.

Unit 3: Review

A. 1. They'll stretch out of shape.   2. They can shrink.   3. how to clean it   4. dampen first; be careful of iron temperature   5. Wash it by hand.

B. Possible answers: 1. sweater   2. soak and rinse it   3. shoes   4. dampen it

C. Possible answers: 1. Pat it flat; fold on seams and waistband if possible.   2. Read the care label.

UNIT 4: HOME MAINTENANCE AND DECORATING

Lesson 1: A Cleaning Schedule

THINKING IT OVER: 1. a   2. b   3. c   4. b

KEY VOCABULARY: 1. share living quarters   2. set times   3. timetable   4. take turns doing them

EVERYDAY MATH: 2 hours, 19 minutes

EXTEND THE LESSON: Possible answers: clean mirrors, wash windows, dust blinds

ON YOUR OWN: Answers will vary.

Lesson 2: Directions on Cleaning Products

THINKING IT OVER: 1. color would change   2. might stain the carpet   3. to keep it from setting   4. skin and eyes

EVERYDAY MATH: The 22-ounce bottle is a better

buy. It costs 24¢ an ounce, whereas the 18-ounce bottle costs 27¢ an ounce.

KEY VOCABULARY: 1. does a good job   2. what it's made of   3. can blot up moisture   4. immediately

PUTTING DETAILS IN ORDER: 3, 6, 4, 5, 2, 7, 1

ON YOUR OWN: Possible answer: No. If he lets all spots just sit, they'll be harder, if not impossible, to clean. Also, he has to live with a dirty carpet most of the time. It's a better idea to spot clean as spots occur.

Lesson 3: Hanging Pictures and Taking Care of Plants

THINKING IT OVER: 1. F   2. T   3. F   4. T   5. T   6. T   7. F   8. F   9. T

KEY VOCABULARY: 1. not natural   2. wetness   3. part of the wooden framing   4. harm

CAUSE AND EFFECT: 1. you might damage the plant with rough handling   2. The mirror fell and broke, perhaps pulling part of the wall down with it.

EVERYDAY MATH: 1. 28 to 40 drops   2. about June 15

ON YOUR OWN: Answers will vary.

Lesson 4: Repairing Wallpaper

THINKING IT OVER: 1. b   2. a   3. c   4. b

KEY VOCABULARY: 1. fix   2. dampen   3. glue   4. extra   5. cut   6. thin

EVERYDAY MATH: $128.85

PUTTING DETAILS IN ORDER: 3, 2, 4, 5, 1

ON YOUR OWN: Answers will vary.

Unit 4: Review

A. Possible answers: 1. DAILY: make bed, wipe kitchen counter; WEEKLY: vacuum carpeting, dust furniture   2. ADVANTAGES: keeps stains from setting, keeps carpet looking good; DISADVANTAGES: product is harmful to eyes and skin, and is toxic in landfills   3. keep them away from heat; keep them away from dampness; use a stud or a molly bolt for the nail   4. moisten the area, cut a v-shaped slit in the bubble, force glue through slit   5. repot in a bigger pot

B. 1. take turns doing them   2. blots

moisture   3. moisture or wetness   4. adhesive

C. Possible answer: find out its light and water needs and then provide them

—BOOK 3—
HEALTH AND SAFETY

UNIT 1: PREVENTION: THE BEST CURE

Lesson 1: Physical Fitness

THINKING IT OVER: 1. a   2. b   3. b   4. c

KEY VOCABULARY: 1. aerobic   2. stress   3. calories

EVERYDAY MATH: yes

COMPARING: 1. running   2. swimming   3. taking a walk

ON YOUR OWN: Answers will vary.

Lesson 2: Hygiene

THINKING IT OVER: 1. T   2. T   3. F   4. F   5. T

KEY VOCABULARY: 1. a   2. b   3. a   4. b   5. c

CAUSE AND EFFECT: 1. you are likely to spread your germs to other people   2. practicing poor dental hygiene   3. bad breath

ON YOUR OWN: Answers will vary.

Lesson 3: Nutrition

THINKING IT OVER: 1. c   2. b   3. c   4. b

EVERYDAY MATH: 1. 2   2. 1

KEY VOCABULARY: 1. United States Department of Agriculture   2. tablespoon   3. Food and Drug Administration   4. DV

COMPARING: 1. more   2. less   3. more

ON YOUR OWN: Answers will vary.

Lesson 4: Staying Safe at Home

THINKING IT OVER: 1.–2. Answers will vary. 3. possible answers: turn pot handles to the back of stove; don't use water on a grease fire

KEY VOCABULARY: 1. accident   2. extinguisher   3. appliances   4. hazard

RECALLING DETAILS: 1. slipping and falling   2. put it out   3. toward the back of the stove   4. pills; cleaning supplies   5. your hands are wet

ON YOUR OWN: Answers will vary.

Unit 1: Review

A. Answers will vary.

B. 1. heart   2. food pyramid   3. soap
4. warm up   5. vegetables   6. bathtub

C. Answers will vary.

UNIT 2: GETTING MEDICAL ATTENTION

Lesson 1: Health Insurance

THINKING IT OVER: 1. b   2. c   3. a   4. c

EVERYDAY MATH: 1. $100   2. $150

KEY VOCABULARY: 1. policy   2. deductible
3. claim   4. Premiums

ON YOUR OWN: Answers will vary.

Lesson 2: The Doctor's Office

THINKING IT OVER: 1. b   2. c   3. b   4. a

KEY VOCABULARY: 1. arteries   2. referral
3. specialist   4. Antibiotics

PUTTING DETAILS IN ORDER: 4, 5, 1, 2, 3

ON YOUR OWN: Answers will vary.

Lesson 3: Dental Treatment

THINKING IT OVER: 1. F   2. T   3. T   4. T   5. F   6.
F   7. T   8. F   9. T

EVERYDAY MATH: six months

KEY VOCABULARY: 1. feeling   2. straightening
teeth   3. cosmetic   4. Fluoride

RECALLING DETAILS: 1. b   2. c   3. b

ON YOUR OWN: Answers will vary.

Lesson 4: Mental Health

THINKING IT OVER: 1. breathing deeply
2. reduce   3. talk about your problems
4. common

RECALLING DETAILS: 1. write   2. answers might
include any of these: school teachers or
counselors, family members, religious
leaders, family doctor

KEY VOCABULARY: 1. emotions   2. therapist
3. journal

IDIOMS: 1. a   2. b   3. b

ON YOUR OWN: Answers will vary.

Unit 2: Review

A. Answers will vary.

B. 1. pediatrician   2. orthodontist
3. stress   4. X-ray

C. Answers will vary.

UNIT 3: HANDLING HEALTH PROBLEMS

Lesson 1: Recognizing Warning Signs

THINKING IT OVER: 1. b   2. a   3. c   4. a

EVERYDAY MATH: 1. above   2. yes   3. 1°

KEY VOCABULARY: 1. T   2. F   3. T   4. F   5. T

COMPARE AND CONTRAST: Answers will vary.

ON YOUR OWN: Answers will vary.

Lesson 2: Quick Action: First Aid and
the Emergency Room

THINKING IT OVER: 1. a   2. c   3. b   4. a   5. a

ABBREVIATIONS: 1. emergency medical services
2. emergency room

KEY VOCABULARY: Seizures

RECALLING DETAILS: •Emergency room visits are
expensive. •The wait in an emergency room
is usually long.

MAKING JUDGMENTS: 1. FA   2. FA   3. 9-1-1
4. ER   5. 9-1-1

ON YOUR OWN: Answers will vary.

Lesson 3: Prescription Medicines

THINKING IT OVER: 1. F   2. T   3. F   4. T   5. T

KEY VOCABULARY: 1. prescription   2. dosage
3. side effects   4. expiration   5. pharmacist
6. pharmacy   7. generic

EVERYDAY MATH: 1. a   2. b   3. a

ON YOUR OWN: Answers will vary.

Lesson 4: Over-the-Counter Medicines

THINKING IT OVER: 1. c   2. a   3. a   4. b

MAKING COMPARISONS: Answers will vary.

INFORMAL LANGUAGE: rule of thumb

ON YOUR OWN: Answers will vary.

Unit 3: Review

A. Answers will vary.

B. 1. allergy   2. prescription
3. pharmacist   4. side effects

C. Answers will vary.

UNIT 4: AVOIDING HEALTH HAZARDS

Lesson 1: Resisting Peer Pressure

THINKING IT OVER: 1. c   2. b   3. c   4. a

KEY VOCABULARY: 1. peer   2. assert   3. negative
4. Tattoos

Saddleback Lifeskills • Saddleback Publishing, Inc., Three Watson, Irvine, CA 92618 • Phone: (888) 735-2225 • Fax: (888) 734-4010 • www.sdlback.com

INFORMAL LANGUAGE: cave in

SUMMARIZING: Answers will vary.

ON YOUR OWN: Answers will vary.

Lesson 2: Tobacco

THINKING IT OVER: 1. T   2. F   3. T   4. F   5. T   6. F

KEY VOCABULARY: 1. addiction   2. Nicotine   3. endurance

EVERYDAY MATH: 1. 20%   2. age 36

SUPPORTING DETAILS: Answers will vary.

ON YOUR OWN: Answers will vary.

Lesson 3: Alcohol and Illegal Drugs

THINKING IT OVER: 1. a   2. b   3. b   4. c

RECALLING DETAILS: 1. alcohol use   2. Answers will vary.   3. any age   4. Answers will vary.

CAUSE AND EFFECT: Answers will vary.

ON YOUR OWN: Answers will vary.

Lesson 4: Infectious Diseases

THINKING IT OVER: 1. a   2. c   3. c   4. a

KEY VOCABULARY: 1. Antibiotics   2. sterile   3. risky   4. saliva

RECALLING DETAILS: 1. V   2. B   3. V

SYNONYMS: 1. ailment   2. contagious   3. catch

ON YOUR OWN: Answers will vary.

Unit 4: Review

A. Answers will vary.

B. 1. Nicotine   2. Drinking alcohol   3. Alcoholism   4. HIV

C. Answers will vary.

—BOOK 4—
MANAGING MONEY

UNIT 1: CONTROLLING YOUR SPENDING

Lesson 1: Developing Thrifty Habits

THINKING IT OVER: 1. a   2. c   3. b   4. a

KEY VOCABULARY: 1. habit   2. Peer pressure   3. frugal   4. debt

EVERYDAY MATH: $6.25

CAUSE AND EFFECT: 1. convince you to spend   2. you'll spend unwisely

ON YOUR OWN: Answers will vary.

Lesson 2: Balancing Wants and Needs

THINKING IT OVER: 1. T   2. T   3. F   4. F   5. T

KEY VOCABULARY: 1. bargain   2. expense   3. buy

EVERYDAY MATH: $552.50

COMPARING: 1. school supplies   2. fingernail polish   3. breakfast food

ON YOUR OWN: Answers will vary.

Lesson 3: Keeping Financial Records

THINKING IT OVER: 1. put into   2. receipts   3. register   4. save

EVERYDAY MATH: 1. $3.00   2. 13 weeks   3. $9.75 entertainment

KEY VOCABULARY: 1. document   2. withdrawal   3. refund   4. balance

DRAWING CONCLUSIONS: Check 1, 3, and 4.

ON YOUR OWN: Answers will vary.

Lesson 4: Common Financial Mistakes

THINKING IT OVER: Check 1, 3, and 5.

EVERYDAY MATH: 1. 32¢   2. $2.28

CAUSE AND EFFECT: 1. late   2. correct bank errors   3. prove

KEY VOCABULARY: 1. a   2. c   3. a   4. b

ON YOUR OWN: Answers will vary.

Unit 1: Review

A. Answers will vary.

B. 1. frugal   2. necessary   3. statement   4. debt

UNIT 2: BANKING BASICS

Lesson 1: Choosing a Bank

THINKING IT OVER: 1. b   2. a   3. b

EVERYDAY MATH: 1a. $7.50   1b. $10.50   2. regular checking, $3.00

KEY VOCABULARY: 1. fees   2. branches

CAUSE AND EFFECT: 1. because it would earn interest   2. George's account paid lower interest than Sabrina's.

ON YOUR OWN: Answers will vary.

Lesson 2: Checking Account and Check Register

THINKING IT OVER: 1. b   2. c   3. a

KEY VOCABULARY: 1. transaction   2. fines   3. overdraw

IDIOMATIC EXPRESSIONS: 1. a   2. a

EVERYDAY MATH: 1. $438.28   2. $63.28   3. no

ON YOUR OWN: Answers will vary.

Lesson 3: Monthly Bank Statement

THINKING IT OVER: 1. all account transactions
2. subtract   3. match   4. more

EVERYDAY MATH: 1. $129.22   2. more

KEY VOCABULARY: 1. ending   2. deposited
3. withdrawals   4. customer

COMPARING: 1. b   2. a

ON YOUR OWN: Answers will vary.

Lesson 4: Savings Accounts

THINKING IT OVER: 1. c   2. b   3. c   4. a

KEY VOCABULARY: 1. bad check   2. interest
3. variable   4. fixed

EVERYDAY MATH: 1. $61.50   2. $46.00

COMPARING: 1. long-term   2. large
3. time deposit   4. start-up

ON YOUR OWN: Answers will vary.

Unit 2: Review

A. Answers will vary.

B. 1. deduct   2. statement   3. ATM
4. time deposit   5. overdraft

C. Answers will vary.

UNIT 3: BUY NOW, PAY LATER

Lesson 1: Dangers of Debt

THINKING IT OVER: 1. T   2. F   3. T   4. F   5. T   6. F   7. T   8. T

KEY VOCABULARY: 1. owe   2. borrow   3. fines
4. investments   5. responsible   6. risks

EVERYDAY MATH: 1. $299.50   2. $57.00

RECALLING DETAILS: 1. c   2. a   3. a

ON YOUR OWN: Answers will vary.

Lesson 2: Using Credit Cards

THINKING IT OVER: 1. T   2. F   3. T   4. F   5. T

KEY VOCABULARY: 1. once a year   2. latest
3. least   4. grace period

CAUSE AND EFFECT: 1. b   2. a   3. c

EVERYDAY MATH: $55.60

ON YOUR OWN: Answers will vary.

Lesson 3: Borrowing Money

THINKING IT OVER: 1. c   2. b   3. c   4. b

KEY VOCABULARY: 1. finance   2. principal
3. down payment   4. income

EVERYDAY MATH: $1,584.00

COMPARING: 1. less   2. more   3. Banks
4. early

ON YOUR OWN: Answers will vary.

Lesson 4: Installment Purchases

THINKING IT OVER: Possible answers:
1. You could lose both your money and your purchase if a store goes out of business or you miss a payment.   2. If stolen or damaged, you still must pay. Your purchase would be repossessed if you got behind on payments.   3. The interest is very high.

EVERYDAY MATH: 1. $2,554.92   2. $1,314.92
3. yes

KEY VOCABULARY: 1. layaway   2. rent-to-own
3. repossess   4. refund

CAUSE AND EFFECT: 1. she lost the gown and her $90.   2. store took the furniture back

ON YOUR OWN: Answers will vary.

Unit 3: Review

A. Possible answers: 1. Debt costs money. You must give up things to pay off debts.   2. You will have to pay late payment fees. You could ruin your credit rating.   3. This lowers the principal and saves you money on interest.   4. Failing to pay bills on time. Not making regular payments on debt.

B. 1. emergencies   2. interest   3. risk
4. income   5. rent-to-own

C. Possible answers:
•What are the monthly payments?
•How many monthly payments are there?
•What is the interest or finance charge?
•Is there a fine for paying the loan off early?

UNIT 4: IMPROVING YOUR BUDGETING SKILLS

Lesson 1: Your Goal: A Balanced Budget

THINKING IT OVER: 1. a   2. c   3. c   4. b

KEY VOCABULARY: 1. fixed   2. variable
3. expected   4. earnings

EVERYDAY MATH: 1. Her expenses are less than her earnings.   2. $230.50

COMPARING: 1. entertainment   2. school supplies
3. her loan payment

ON YOUR OWN: Answers will vary.

Lesson 2: Keeping a Personal Expense Record

THINKING IT OVER: 1. b   2. c   3. b   4. b

KEY VOCABULARY: 1. spending more than you can afford   2. personal expense record
3. category   4. variable

EVERYDAY MATH: Circle *snack food: $9.50, movie/popcorn: $12.65, game tokens: $15.75,* and *comic store purchases: $29.82.*
Total savings: $67.72

CLASSIFYING: 1. Laundry   2. Personal Care
3. Entertainment

ON YOUR OWN: Answers will vary.

Lesson 3: Typical Budget Adjustments

THINKING IT OVER: 1. a   2. b   3. c   4. c

KEY VOCABULARY: 1. adjust   2. subtract   3. repair
4. reduce

EVERYDAY MATH: yes

MAKING JUDGMENTS: Answers will vary.

ON YOUR OWN: Answers will vary.

Lesson 4: Handling Unexpected Expenses

THINKING IT OVER: 1. b   2. c   3. a   4. c

KEY VOCABULARY: 1. predict   2. unexpected
3. collateral   4. reduce

EVERYDAY MATH: $44.64

DRAWING CONCLUSIONS: 1. You cannot change or control the amount you must pay each month.   2. to make sure she paid back her loan in a year and didn't lose money from her savings

ON YOUR OWN: Answers will vary.

Unit 4: Review

A. 1., 2., and 4. Answers will vary.
3. Fixed expenses stay the same and/or must be paid every month. Variable expenses can be reduced, increased, or delayed.

B. 1. expected   2. equal   3. adjustment
4. collateral   5. monthly

C. Answers will vary.

—BOOK 5—
CONSUMER SPENDING

UNIT 1: THE WISE BUYER

Lesson 1: Principles of Smart Shopping

THINKING IT OVER: Circle 2, 3, 5, 6, 7, 8, and 10.

KEY VOCABULARY: 1. f   2. a   3. e   4. c   5. d   6. b

EVERYDAY MATH: 1. $7.50   2. No. Two pairs would cost $123 at his regular store. He'd save $24 on two pairs from The Eye Site.

ON YOUR OWN: Answers will vary.

Lesson 2: Interpreting Ad Copy

THINKING IT OVER: 1. b   2. c   3. b   4. a

KEY VOCABULARY: 1. prove   2. feels
3. comparatives   4. exaggerate
5. misleading

EVERYDAY MATH: $27.99

FACT VS. OPINION: 1. O   2. F   3. O   4. O   5. F
6. O   7. F   8. F

ON YOUR OWN: Answers will vary.

Lesson 3: Avoiding Unexpected Costs

THINKING IT OVER: 1. T   2. F   3. T   4. F   5. T   6. T

KEY VOCABULARY: 1. guess   2. agree to have the work done and pay for it   3. signature

RECALLING DETAILS: Circle 1, 3, and 4.

EVERYDAY MATH: 1. $916.34   2. $225.00
3. $58.69   4. $1,136.79

ON YOUR OWN: Answers will vary.

Lesson 4: In Search of Bargains

THINKING IT OVER: 1. N   2. U   3. N   4. U   5. U
6. N   7. U   8. U

KEY VOCABULARY: 1. something selling at a greatly lowered price   2. the item is slightly damaged or missing something like a button
3. buy the item for less than the price the seller is asking   4. not quite perfect

EVERYDAY MATH: 1. $137.50   2. $107

DRAWING CONCLUSIONS: 1. c   2. c

ON YOUR OWN: Answers will vary.

Unit 1: Review

A. 1. wait until the items go on sale
2. Discount stores sell things for less but may not offer good service.
3. Prices change depending on the season and how long the item has been for sale.   4. Accept all reasonable answers.

B. 1. compare   2. exaggerate
3. authorizing   4. and 5. Accept all reasonable answers.

C. Answers will vary, but could include: Learn about the product; compare different brands and prices; consider your wants and needs.

UNIT 2: SHOPPING FOR GOODS

Lesson 1: Return Policies

THINKING IT OVER: 1. a   2. c   3. b

KEY VOCABULARY: 1. refund   2. goods
3. defective   4. policies   5. trade

EVERYDAY MATH: 1. $3.99   2. $7

RECALLING DETAILS: 1. F   2. F   3. T   4. F   5. F

ON YOUR OWN: Answers will vary.

Lesson 2: Buying Household Goods

THINKING IT OVER: 3, 1, 4, 5, 2

KEY VOCABULARY: 1. important   2. and 3. Accept any reasonable answer.   4. easy to use

EVERYDAY MATH: 1. $80   2. $6.50   3. $35

MAKING DECISIONS: Answers will vary.

ON YOUR OWN: Answers will vary.

Lesson 3: Assembling a Wardrobe

THINKING IT OVER: 1. b   2. c   3. c   4. b

KEY VOCABULARY: Accept all reasonable answers. 1. All the clothes you wear.
2. The things you do most of the time.
3. clothing material   4. won't wash out

EVERYDAY MATH: Accept all reasonable answers.

CAUSE AND EFFECT: 1. S   2. W   3. S   4. W   5. S

ON YOUR OWN: Answers will vary.

Lesson 4: Shopping from Home

THINKING IT OVER: 1. TV, phone, computer, mail order   2. check, money order, credit card
3.–5. Accept all reasonable answers.

KEY VOCABULARY: 1. how many or how much
2. buying from the place where the item is made   3. examine or check the item for defects   4. one single item

CAUSE AND EFFECT: 1. No. He has no proof he paid for the book.   2. a. copy of order form, charge and bill, catalog ad   b. Yes, if she shows her proof to the company and reports the error to her credit card company.

EVERYDAY MATH: $84; $8.40; $92.40

ON YOUR OWN: Answers will vary.

Unit 2: Review

A.   Accept any reasonable answer.
1. show proof of purchase; return the item immediately or within a week
2. This helps you decide what to buy now and what to get later.
3. convenience; worldwide stores; savings on prices

B. 1. you can't get a cash refund, but you can trade in the item for store credit
2. features   3. fabric   4. shipping
5. restocking

C. Answers will vary.

UNIT 3: SHOPPING FOR SERVICES

Lesson 1: Checking Out Reputations and References

THINKING IT OVER: Circle 1, 3, 4, and 5.

KEY VOCABULARY: Accept all reasonable answers. 1. is trained or experienced in a specific occupation   2. to direct attention to   3. to praise another as being worthy   4. to be held in high regard by the public

EVERYDAY MATH: 1. $200   2. $70   3. $25

MAKING JUDGMENTS: 1. no   2. yes   3. no
4. no   5. yes   6. no   7. no   8. no

ON YOUR OWN: Answers will vary.

Lesson 2: Comparing Life Insurance Policies

THINKING IT OVER: 1. to protect dependents
2. The policy could lapse.   3. different face value or age of insured   4. You wouldn't be covered.

KEY VOCABULARY: 1. d   2. c   3. e   4. f   5. b   6. a

EVERYDAY MATH: 1. a. $7.10 b. 10 c. $71
2. a. $17.10 b. 40 c. $684

ON YOUR OWN: Answers will vary.

Lesson 3: Comparing Cable TV Services

THINKING IT OVER: 1. c 2. b 3. a

KEY VOCABULARY: Accept all reasonable answers.
1. to place or adjust in a specific position for use 2. a receptable usually mounted on the wall and connected to a power source and equipped with a socket for a plug

EVERYDAY MATH: 1. $57.96 2. $39.98 3. $13

ON YOUR OWN: Answers will vary.

Lesson 4: Hiring a Pro vs. Doing It Yourself

THINKING IT OVER: Circle 1, 2, 4, 6, and 7.

KEY VOCABULARY: Accept all reasonable answers.
1. space for air to circulate and dissipate 2. paint stripper, solvents 3. be careful to avoid an accident and/or injury

EVERYDAY MATH: 1. $38.93 2. $28.93

DECISION MAKING: 1.–3. Accept all reasonable answers.

ON YOUR OWN: Answers will vary.

Unit 3: Review

A. 1.–4. Answers will vary.
B. 1. estimates 2. premiums
3. dividends 4. install 5. guarantee
C. Answers will vary.

UNIT 4: CONSUMER RIGHTS

Lesson 1: Credit Card Benefits

THINKING IT OVER: 1.–4. Answers will vary.

KEY VOCABULARY: 1. rebate 2. extended warranty
3. disagree with the charge 4. pay for the charges

EVERYDAY MATH: 1. 8¢ 2. $1.52 3. 4¢

CAUSE AND EFFECT: Answers will vary.

ON YOUR OWN: Answers will vary.

Lesson 2: Making Complaints

THINKING IT OVER: 1. solved, or remedied
2. receipt, bill, canceled check, estimate
3. write a complaint letter 4. BBB

KEY VOCABULARY: 1. a buyer 2. solution or settlement

EVERYDAY MATH: 1. $3.90 2. $11.70

FOLLOWING DIRECTIONS: July 22, 2003; 442A; B10354; July 24, 2003; $35.39; $249.67; 650-555-5334; Lydia M. Sanchez

ON YOUR OWN: Answers will vary.

Lesson 3: Warranties

THINKING IT OVER: 1.–3. Answers will vary.

KEY VOCABULARY: 1. guarantees 2. Limited
3. extended 4. implied 5. obligations

EVERYDAY MATH: 1. $255 2. No. The warranty has cost Matt $129.02 more than the cost of repairs.

COMPARING: 1. b 2. b

ON YOUR OWN: Answers will vary.

Lesson 4: Telemarketing and Trial Offers

THINKING IT OVER: 1. a 2. c 3. b

KEY VOCABULARY: 1. telemarketer 2. scam
3. cancel

EVERYDAY MATH: No. She was paying $1.31 more for the books from the mail order club.

MAKING JUDGMENTS: Check 1, 2, 4, and 6.

ON YOUR OWN: Answers will vary.

Unit 4: Review

A. 1.–4. Answers will vary.
B. 1. credit card 2. solution 3. limited
4. implied 5. protection
C. Answers will vary.

—BOOK 6—
JOB SEARCH

UNIT 1: WORKPLACE READINESS

Lesson 1: Aptitudes/Interests Inventory

THINKING IT OVER: 1. b 2. a 3. b 4. a

KEY VOCABULARY: 1. b 2. a 3. d 4. c

RECALLING DETAILS: 1. T 2. T 3. F 4. F

EVERYDAY MATH/CRITICAL THINKING: 1. 5,465 2. no

ON YOUR OWN: Answers will vary.

Lesson 2: Career Categories and Preparation

THINKING IT OVER: 1. c 2. a 3. b 4. a 5. c

RECALLING MAIN IDEAS: 1. T 2. T 3. F 4. T

KEY VOCABULARY: 1. a person who is skilled and experienced in a certain job 2. things sold in stores 3. an office

CATEGORIES: 1. Answers will vary.   2. Answers will vary, but could include carpenter, electrician, plumber, mason.

EVERYDAY MATH: $279.17

ON YOUR OWN: Answers will vary.

Lesson 3: Salaries and Job Benefits

THINKING IT OVER: 1. T   2. F   3. T   4. F

KEY VOCABULARY: 1. b   2. a   3. b   4. a

CAUSE AND EFFECT: 1. pay for all doctor visits, lab tests, hospital stays, and medications   2. nothing or zero   3. money to live on when you retire

EVERYDAY MATH: 1. $480   2. $420   3. Ace Roofing

ON YOUR OWN: Answers will vary.

Lesson 4: Short-Term and Long-Term Goals

THINKING IT OVER: 1. c   2. a   3. b

KEY VOCABULARY: 1. e   2. a   3. b   4. c   5. d

COMPARING: 1. P.J.   2. Erin   3. P.J.

EVERYDAY MATH: 1. $1,400   2. $1,525

ON YOUR OWN: Answers will vary.

Unit 1: Review

A. 1. a trade   2. the government   3. wages   4. aptitude   5. classified   6. profession   7. benefit   8. an apprentice; a journeyman

B. 1. like: opportunity to make unlimited money; dislike: uncertain amount of salary   2. Answers will vary.   3. Answers will vary.

UNIT 2: OCCUPATIONAL TRAINING

Lesson 1: Basic Skills in Business

THINKING IT OVER: 1. a   2. c   3. b

KEY VOCABULARY: 1. boss   2. foundation   3. contract   4. percentage   5. invoice

EVERYDAY MATH: $1,736.07

ON YOUR OWN: 1. to make something happen in an easier or faster way; to speed up or hasten   2. $1,205

Lesson 2: Occupational Training

THINKING IT OVER: 1. a   2. b   3. b   4. a

KEY VOCABULARY: 1. a   2. b   3. a   4. b

NOTING DETAILS: 1. c   2. d   3. b   4. a

EVERYDAY MATH: 3 hours

ON YOUR OWN: Answers will vary.

Lesson 3: Community College

THINKING IT OVER: 1. T   2. T   3. F   4. T   5. T   6. T   7. F

KEY VOCABULARY: 1. a   2. b   3. a

EVERYDAY MATH: $33

CAUSE AND EFFECT: You can transfer to another college at an advanced level. The AA will help you qualify for better jobs.

ON YOUR OWN: Answers will vary.

Lesson 4: On-the-Job Training

THINKING IT OVER: 1. a   2. b   3. c   4. a

RECALLING DETAILS: 1. carpenters' union office   2. GED   3. Labor Organizations   4. good pay and helpful benefits

KEY VOCABULARY: 1. b   2. a   3. c   4. d

EVERYDAY MATH: $248

ON YOUR OWN: Answers will vary.

Unit 2: Review

A. 1. invoices   2. vocational school   3. catalog   4. income   5. speak   6. two   7. unions   8. an intern

B. 1. associate of arts degree   2. a salary   3. General Educational Development

UNIT 3: APPLYING FOR A JOB

Lesson 1: Classified "Help Wanted" Ads

THINKING IT OVER: 1. b   2. c   3. a   4. b

KEY VOCABULARY: 1. b   2. a   3. d   4. e   5. c   6. f

RECALLING DETAILS: 1. fax   2. directly to the workplace   3. Office Asst/Auto Shop   4. Driver/Warehouse Work   5. Customer Service   6. Counter Help   7. Driver/Warehouse

EVERYDAY MATH: $304.25

ON YOUR OWN: Answers will vary.

Lesson 2: Agencies: Private and State

THINKING IT OVER: 1. T   2. F   3. T   4. T   5. T   6. F

KEY VOCABULARY: 1. a   2. b   3. a

RECALLING DETAILS: 1. b 2. b 3. b

EVERYDAY MATH: lifeguard; 15 hours

ON YOUR OWN: Answers will vary.

Lesson 3: Résumé and Cover Letter

THINKING IT OVER: 1. a 2. c 3. a 4. b

KEY VOCABULARY: 1. b 2. a 3. d 4. c 5. e

RECALLING DETAILS: 1. name, address, phone, e-mail 2. 1 or 2 pages

EVERYDAY MATH: $2.16

ON YOUR OWN: Answers will vary.

Lesson 4: Completing a Job Application

THINKING IT OVER: 1. T 2. F 3. F 4. T 5. T

KEY VOCABULARY: 1. allow 2. past 3. swear

DRAWING CONCLUSIONS: 1. number 2. boss 3. convicted 4. yes 5. job 6. yes 7. yes 8. yes; I might need to use the same information again when I fill out other forms

EVERYDAY MATH: 22

ON YOUR OWN: Answers will vary.

Unit 3: Review

A. 1. an application 2. temporary 3. Assistant 4. education 5. part-time 6. agencies 7. Internet 8. called in for an interview

B. 1. to keep good records of your job search 2. at a public library

UNIT 4: THE JOB INTERVIEW

Lesson 1: Businesslike Communication

THINKING IT OVER: 1. a 2. c 3. c 4. a

KEY VOCABULARY: 1. b 2. d 3. a 4. c

SEQUENCING: 2, 1, 4, 5, 3

EVERYDAY MATH: 14

ON YOUR OWN: Answers will vary.

Lesson 2: Dressing for Success

THINKING IT OVER: 1. c 2. a 3. b 4. b 5. c

KEY VOCABULARY: 1. coordinated 2. neat, clean 3. positive

SEQUENCING: 3, 2, 1, 6, 4, 5

EVERYDAY MATH: 1. $13 2. $6

ON YOUR OWN: Answers will vary.

Lesson 3: Answering Questions

THINKING IT OVER: 1. a 2. b 3. c 4. b

EVERYDAY MATH: 1. $66 2. yes

KEY VOCABULARY: 1. a 2. b 3. b 4. a

RECALLING DETAILS: 1. T 2. F 3. T 4. T 5. T

ON YOUR OWN: Answers will vary.

Lesson 4: Follow-up Call, Thank-you Note

THINKING IT OVER: 1. c 2. b 3. a

KEY VOCABULARY: 1. formal 2. interviewer 3. documents 4. contribution

EVERYDAY MATH: $4.50

RECALLING DETAILS: 1. T 2. F 3. F 4. T

ON YOUR OWN: Answers will vary.

Unit 4: Review

A. 1. turned off 2. confidence 3. slowly and clearly 4. neat and clean 5. eyebrow 6. pleasant and courteous 7. former employer 8. contribute

B. smoke, chew gum, tell jokes

C. Answers will vary.

—BOOK 7—
GETTING AHEAD AT WORK

UNIT 1: OFF TO A GOOD START

Lesson 1: The Importance of First Impressions

THINKING IT OVER: 1. F 2. T 3. T 4. T 5. F 6. T 7. F 8. F 9. F

KEY VOCABULARY: 1. b 2. a 3. a 4. b 5. c

EVERYDAY MATH: 65 minutes

ON YOUR OWN: Answers will vary.

Lesson 2: An Employee Handbook

THINKING IT OVER: 1. b 2. a 3. b 4. a 5. b 6. a

EVERYDAY MATH: $393.50

KEY VOCABULARY: 1. e 2. f 3. a 4. b 5. c 6. d

RECALLING DETAILS: shift times, overtime, sick leave, vacations, location of supplies, parking procedures and location, safety precautions, grievance procedures

ON YOUR OWN: Answers will vary.

Lesson 3: Fitting In with Co-Workers

THINKING IT OVER: 1. T 2. F 3. T 4. F 5. F 6. T 7. F 8. F 9. F

KEY VOCABULARY: 1. get more of them weekly or monthly, or at a scheduled time 2. ways of doing things 3. keep yourself from joining in

EVERYDAY MATH: Alternative answers: one $10 bill and three $1 bills; two $5 bills and three $1 bills; 18 $1 bills

ON YOUR OWN: Answers will vary.

Lesson 4: Interpreting a Paycheck

THINKING IT OVER: 1. F 2. F 3. F 4. T 5. F 6. T

KEY VOCABULARY: 1. b 2. b 3. a 4. c 5. b 6. c 7. a

EVERYDAY MATH: $693.45

ON YOUR OWN: 1. Answers will vary. 2. 65

Unit 1: Review

A. 1. reach out to shake hands 2. health insurance 3. Federal Income Tax and Social Security (FICA) 4. It will look like you're taking sides.

B. 1. grievance 2. appropriate 3. employee handbook 4. credit union

C. 1. c 2. d 3. a 4. b

UNIT 2: LEARNING THE JOB

Lesson 1: Impressing Your Supervisor

THINKING IT OVER: 1. a 2. c 3. b 4. b 5. b 6. c 7. b

ANTONYMS: 1. i 2. c 3. a 4. d 5. f 6. b 7. g 8. h 9. e

EVERYDAY MATH: $2,625

ON YOUR OWN: Answers will vary.

Lesson 2: Following Verbal Directions and Asking for Clarification

KEY VOCABULARY: 1. spoken 2. you understand what you're being told 3. simple

THINKING IT OVER: 1. b 2. a 3. c 4. a 5. b 6. a

EVERYDAY MATH: 57

SEQUENCING: 1, 4, 2, 3

ON YOUR OWN: Answers will vary.

Lesson 3: Reading Instructions: Using a Job Aid

THINKING IT OVER: 1. F 2. T 3. F 4. F 5. T 6. T 7. F

KEY VOCABULARY: 1. instructions 2. manual 3. procedures 4. Ergonomics

EVERYDAY MATH: He moved it 4 inches closer and lowered the screen 4 inches.

RECALLING DETAILS: Briona: on the photocopying machine; Jason: in the instruction manual inside the packing crate; Ty: from guidelines given to him by his supervisor

ON YOUR OWN: Answers will vary.

Lesson 4: Teamwork and Cooperation

THINKING IT OVER: 1. F 2. F 3. F 4. T 5. F 6. F 7. T 8. F 9. T

KEY VOCABULARY: 1. do all the talking so no one else has a chance to say anything 2. adjust your ways so they will work with someone else's 3. say something positive about them

SYNONYMS: 1. e 2. a 3. c 4. d 5. b

EVERYDAY MATH: $699,881; $594,376

ON YOUR OWN: Answers will vary.

Unit 2: Review

A. 1. prompt 2. instructions 3. Teamwork 4. written 5. subtracts from 6. notes 7. compliment 8. sequence

B. 1. T 2. T 3. T

C. Answers will vary, but could include: pay attention at meetings, try to do the best job you can, show that you want to learn, etc.

UNIT 3: SUCCEEDING ON THE JOB

Lesson 1: Measurements of Progress

THINKING IT OVER: Underline 1, 3, 4, 8.

KEY VOCABULARY: 1. work without asking someone else for help 2. advance; go forward; make headway; achieve your goals; improve 3. guidelines or rules

EVERYDAY MATH: $60; $210; $150

RECALLING DETAILS: Circle 1, 3, 4, 6, 7, 8.

ON YOUR OWN: Answers will vary.

Lesson 2: Benchmarks: Speed and Accuracy

THINKING IT OVER: 1. F 2. F 3. T 4. T 5. F
6. T 7. T

KEY VOCABULARY: 1. c 2. b 3. e 4. a 5. d

DRAWING CONCLUSIONS: carpenter, fabric salesperson, stone cutter, seamstress, carpet installer

EVERYDAY MATH: 1. 3,240; 360; 120; Kyle

ON YOUR OWN: Answers will vary.

Lesson 3: Taking Initiative

THINKING IT OVER: 1. b 2. a 3. c 4. a

KEY VOCABULARY: 1. need to be told what to do
2. different ways to do the same task
3. depend 4. answers

RECALLING DETAILS: suggested a way to sell more computer cases; set up a file box for the office signs; volunteered his help at the retirement party

EVERYDAY MATH: $69.98; $174.95; $104.97

ON YOUR OWN: Answers will vary.

Lesson 4: Qualifying for a Raise

THINKING IT OVER: 1. F 2. F 3. T 4. F 5. F
6. T 7. F

KEY VOCABULARY: 1. a 2. a 3. c 4. b 5. b
6. c

EVERYDAY MATH: $280

RECALLING DETAILS: the quality of my work; my attendance; my input of ideas (or my extra work); my attitude

ON YOUR OWN: Answers will vary.

Unit 3: Review

A. 1. Answers may be any two of the following: Am I able to work independently? Do I catch and correct my own mistakes? Do I finish on time? Do I have a feeling of accomplishment?
2. speed and accuracy 3. find solutions to problems, create alternative procedures, or volunteer for a task or project

B. 1. negotiate 2. standards or guidelines 3. initiative 4. alternative procedure 5. measure twice, cut once

C. Answers will vary.

UNIT 4: WORKPLACE PROBLEMS AND SOLUTIONS

Lesson 1: Reliability: Tardiness and Absenteeism

THINKING IT OVER: 1. b 2. b 3. a 4. b 5. c

CAUSE AND EFFECT: 1. early enough 2. late
3. time 4. fail 5. schedule

KEY VOCABULARY: 1. d 2. a 3. b 4. c 5. e
6. f

EVERYDAY MATH: 65 minutes; 6:10

ON YOUR OWN: Answers will vary.

Lesson 2: Handling Criticism

THINKING IT OVER: 1. F 2. F 3. T 4. F 5. F
6. T 7. T 8. T 9. T 10. F

KEY VOCABULARY: 1. c 2. e 3. a 4. d 5. b

RECALLING DETAILS/SEQUENCING: 4, 1, 2, 3, 5

EVERYDAY MATH: $31,620

ON YOUR OWN: Answers will vary.

Lesson 3: Personal Problems Carried into the Workplace

THINKING IT OVER: 1. c 2. c 3. c 4. b 5. b

KEY VOCABULARY: 1. do good work 2. good; an advantage

DRAWING CONCLUSIONS: Circle 1, 2, 4.

EVERYDAY MATH: 128

ON YOUR OWN: Answers will vary.

Lesson 4: Relationships with Co-Workers

THINKING IT OVER: 1. F 2. F 3. T 4. F 5. F
6. T 7. T 8. F

KEY VOCABULARY: 1. criticize 2. unfamiliar 3. cope
4. belief 5. respect 6. tradition 7. gender

EVERYDAY MATH: 36; 24; 48; 6

ON YOUR OWN: Answers will vary.

Unit 4: Review

A. 1. accept them and attempt to understand them; try to learn from them; get information about their traditions; show the person respect
2. family problems, money problems, relationships with boyfriends or girlfriends 3. report it to your supervisor; file a complaint

B. 1. gender 2. tardy 3. traditions
4. respect

C. Answers will vary, but should include: Worst—get angry; defend poor work; ignore the problem; criticize your supervisor   Best—turn the criticism into something positive; make constructive changes in procedures; find solutions to workplace problems

—BOOK 8—
COMMUNITY RESOURCES

UNIT 1: YOUR TAXES AT WORK

Lesson 1: Public Resources

THINKING IT OVER: 1. T   2. F   3. T   4. F

RECALLING DETAILS ON THE CHART: 1. animal control   2. passports   3. public transportation   4. poison control hotline   5. crime prevention   6. highways

KEY VOCABULARY: 1. veteran   2. Recycling   3. passport   4. Chamber of Commerce   5. Medicare

ON YOUR OWN: Answers will vary.

Lesson 2: Library Services

THINKING IT OVER: Answers will vary.

SUMMARIZING: Answers will vary.

KEY VOCABULARY: 1. branches   2. CD   3. DVD   4. reference

RECALLING DETAILS: checkmark by 3, 6, 9, and 10

ON YOUR OWN: Answers will vary.

Lesson 3: Post Office Services

THINKING IT OVER: 1. c   2. b   3. b   4. a

KEY VOCABULARY: 1. parcel   2. express   3. fragile   4. confirmation   5. periodical   6. via

EVERYDAY MATH: 1. $2.67   2. $13.28

ON YOUR OWN: Answers will vary.

Lesson 4: Parks and Recreation

THINKING IT OVER: checkmark by 1, 2, 4, 6, 7, 9, and 12

RECALLING DETAILS: 1. sight, smell, sound   2. answers include: whack, chat, buzz, cheers, shouts, bubbling   3. answers include: tennis, off-leash dog area, softball, jogging trail, picnicking, wedding facilities   4. late afternoon   5. sunny

IN YOUR OPINION: Answers will vary.

KEY VOCABULARY: 1. gymnasium   2. Toddlers are younger.   3. wedding vows

ON YOUR OWN: Answers will vary.

Unit 1: Review

A. Answers will vary.

B. 1. Medicare   2. Express   3. Parks and Recreation   4. taxes

C. Answers will vary.

UNIT 2: EMERGENCY ASSISTANCE

Lesson 1: Emergency Medical Services

THINKING IT OVER: 1. b   2. c   3. a   4. c

KEY VOCABULARY: 1. technician   2. dispatcher   3. ambulance   4. transcript

ABBREVIATIONS: 1. emergency medical services   2. emergency medical technician

MAKING INFERENCES: Answers will vary.

ON YOUR OWN: Answers will vary.

Lesson 2: Police and Fire Department Services

THINKING IT OVER: 1. b   2. a   3. b   4. c   5. a

KEY VOCABULARY: 1. mission   2. Pedestrians   3. Firefighter   4. Arson

RECALLING DETAILS: 1. under 18   2. They find people lost in the wilderness.   3. They check to see if buildings meet fire codes.

INFORMAL LANGUAGE: hand-in-hand

ON YOUR OWN: Answers will vary.

Lesson 3: Help in a Crisis: Hotlines and Shelters

THINKING IT OVER: 1. National Hotline for Missing Children, Child Find Hotline   2. Children of Alcoholics Foundation   3. Dial-A-Teacher

KEY VOCABULARY: 1. crisis   2. referral   3. volunteer   4. abuse   5. shelter

A CLOSER LOOK: Answers will vary.

RECALLING DETAILS: 1. 1-800   2. Answers will vary.

ON YOUR OWN: Answers will vary.

Lesson 4: Legal Aid and Public Defenders

THINKING IT OVER: 1. T   2. F   3. T   4. T   5. F   6. F

KEY VOCABULARY: 1. lawyer, attorney   2. landlord   3. tenant   4. accused

WORD FORMS: 1. defend 2. defender
  3. defendant

DRAWING CONCLUSIONS: Answers will vary.

ON YOUR OWN: Answers will vary.

Unit 2: Review

- **A.** 1. 9-1-1 2. fire department
  3. low income, disabled, senior citizens
  4., 5., and 6. Answers will vary.
- **B.** 1. hotlines 2. legal aid 3. public
  defender 4. juvenile officer
- **C.** Answers will vary.

UNIT 3: SERVICES FOR WORKERS

Lesson 1: Getting a Social Security Card

THINKING IT OVER: 1. c 2. c 3. b 4. c

RECALLING DETAILS: retirement, unemployment,
disability, death

KEY VOCABULARY: 1. d 2. e 3. c 4. b
  5. f 6. a

ON YOUR OWN: Answers will vary.

Lesson 2: State Employment Office

THINKING IT OVER: 1. T 2. F 3. F 4. T 5. T

KEY VOCABULARY: 1. b 2. b 3. a

INFORMAL LANGUAGE: 1. terminated 2. live on
while job hunting 3. pay bills and buy
necessities

RECALLING DETAILS: provide unemployment
insurance payments; provide lists of job
openings; match a job seeker's skills with
jobs; give information on job training,
interview techniques, and résumé writing

ON YOUR OWN: Answers will vary.

Lesson 3: Federal Safeguards

THINKING IT OVER: 1. a 2. c 3. c 4. b

KEY VOCABULARY: 1. enforce 2. Violations
  3. comply

COMPARING: 1. ESA 2. OSHA 3. OSHA
  4. ESA 5. OSHA

ON YOUR OWN: Answers will vary.

Lesson 4: Filing for Worker's Compensation

THINKING IT OVER: 1. T 2. T 3. F 4. T 5. F

KEY VOCABULARY: 1. Compensation 2. gender
  3. Physical therapy 4. denied

RECALLING DETAILS: 1. broke his ankle on the job
  2. receive Workers' Compensation benefits

EVERYDAY MATH: 1. $400 2. $1,600

ON YOUR OWN: Answers will vary.

Unit 3: Review

- **A.** 1. It helps Americans meet financial
  needs when they are no longer
  working. 2. provide unemployment
  insurance payments; provide lists of job
  openings; match a job seekers skills with
  jobs; give information on job training,
  interview techniques, and résumé writing
  3. They check to see that workplaces
  meet safety and health standards.
  4. Workers file for Worker's Compensation if
  they are injured on the job or become
  sick because of working conditions.
  5. •Workers' Compensation •because you
  need to have a Social Security card
  before you can receive payment for work
- **B.** hospital record of birth, baptismal
  record, driver's license, passport,
  adoption record, military record, school
  ID card, Certificate of Citizenship or of
  Naturalization
- **C.** name, gender, Social Security number,
  mailing address, date of birth,
  occupation or job title, description of
  accident, home and/or work phone
  number, type of injury/disease and part
  of body it affected, date of injury or
  disease

UNIT 4: SERVICES FOR CITIZENS

Lesson 1: Vital Records

THINKING IT OVER: 1. F 2. T 3. T 4. F 5. F

KEY VOCABULARY: 1. Vital 2. certificate
  3. certified 4. maiden name 5. deceased

WHAT IF? Yes. States typically restrict access to
birth records for only 100 years and death
certificates for only 50 years.

EVERYDAY MATH: 1. 82 2. no 3. yes

ON YOUR OWN: Answers will vary.

Lesson 2: The Right to Vote

THINKING IT OVER: 1. a 2. b 3. a 4. c 5. a

KEY VOCABULARY: 1. polls 2. ballots 3. precinct 4. party

EVERYDAY MATH: 2005

RECALLING DETAILS: 1. 1971, amendment 2. Possible answers: Constitution, Democratic, Libertarian, Reform, Pacific Green, Republican

ON YOUR OWN: Answers will vary.

Lesson 3: Legal Immigration: The INS and Green Cards

THINKING IT OVER: 1. b 2. a 3. b 4. a

KEY VOCABULARY: 1. native 2. visa 3. aliens 4. deported

SYNONYMS: 1. qualified 2. guard 3. wife

RECALLING DETAILS: by marrying a U.S. citizen; through his or her employer

ON YOUR OWN: Answers will vary.

Lesson 4: Becoming a Citizen

THINKING IT OVER: 1. c 2. a 3. c 4. b

KEY VOCABULARY: ritual, promise, loyalty, vow

EVERYDAY MATH: 1. 6 years 2. 1 3. 5

MAKING INFERENCES: 1. Yes, because she took English lessons and in high school, U.S. history was her favorite subject. 2. yes

PUTTING EVENTS IN ORDER: 3, 1, 5, 4, 2

ON YOUR OWN: Answers will vary.

Unit 4: Review

A. 1. birth, death, marriage 2. proof of age, proof of citizenship 3. at least 18 years old and a U.S. citizen 4. birth, naturalization 5. register with your election bureau

B. 1. maiden name 2. ballot 3. Green Card 4. oath of allegiance

C. 1. EB 2. DVS 3. INS 4. INS 5. DVS 6. INS 7. DVS

—BOOK 9—
PUBLIC TRANSPORTATION AND TRAVEL

UNIT 1: COMMUTING TO SCHOOL AND WORK

Lesson 1: The Dangers of Hitchhiking

THINKING IT OVER: 1. b 2. b 3. c 4. a

KEY VOCABULARY: 1. danger 2. driver 3. outcomes 4. horrible 5. inexpensive 6. honest

DRAWING CONCLUSIONS: Answers will vary.

ANTONYMS: 1. d 2. e 3. b 4. f 5. c 6. a

ON YOUR OWN: Answers will vary

Lesson 2: Taking the Ankle Express: Walking

THINKING IT OVER: 1. F 2. T 3. T 4. T 5. F

KEY VOCABULARY: 1. A stroll is a leisurely walk, while a race-walk is almost a run. 2. RW 3. S 4. RW 5. S 6. RW

RECALLING DETAILS: 1. walking 2. talk, sing 3. and 4. Answers will vary. 5. the U.S. Surgeon General

INFORMAL LANGUAGE: Answers will vary, but will probably mention walking.

ON YOUR OWN: Answers will vary.

Lesson 3: Biking: The Rules of the Road

THINKING IT OVER: 1. T 2. F 3. F 4. F 5. T

KEY VOCABULARY: 1. defensive 2. anticipate 3. tandem

WORKING WITH SUFFIXES: 1. a. bicyclist b. motorist 2. a. rider b. driver

PLAYING WITH WORDS: Wanda's Whirled of Wheels, whirled

DRAWING CONCLUSIONS: 1. a 2. a 3. a 4. a

ON YOUR OWN: Answers will vary.

Lesson 4: Ride Sharing: Going My Way?

THINKING IT OVER: 1. a 2. b 3. c 4. b

KEY VOCABULARY: 1. van 2. a group of people working together for a common benefit 3. hassle 4. wear and tear

RECALLING DETAILS: 1. car sharing 2. carpooling 3. by reducing traffic and/or air pollution

EVERYDAY MATH: 1. $720 2. $158

ON YOUR OWN: Answers will vary.

Unit 1: Review

A. Answers will vary.

B. 1. to hitchhike; to stick out your thumb as a signal that you want a ride 2. a bike specially built for two riders 3. car share

C. Answers will vary.

D. Answers will vary.

Saddleback Lifeskills • Saddleback Publishing, Inc.,Three Watson, Irvine, CA 92618 • Phone: (888) 735-2225 • Fax: (888) 734-4010 • www.sdlback.com

UNIT 2: TRAVELING BY BUS

Lesson 1: The Benefits of Public Transportation

THINKING IT OVER: 1. a 2. b 3. a 4. b 5. a

KEY VOCABULARY: 1. Urban 2. route 3. subway 4. accessible 5. Congestion

RECALLING DETAILS: 1. lifts for wheelchairs; Braille signs for the blind 2. less traffic congestion; less air pollution 3. special bus lanes; fareless squares

ON YOUR OWN: Answers will vary.

Lesson 2: Using a Route Map

THINKING IT OVER: 1. a 2. b 3. c

KEY VOCABULARY: 1. destination 2. station 3. convenient

USE THE MAP: 1. a 2. c 3. a 4. a. 4th and Empire Blvd. b. 9th Street Transit Center c. no d. yes 5. yes; light rail 6. a

ON YOUR OWN: Answers will vary.

Lesson 3: A Bus Schedule

THINKING IT OVER: 1. T 2. F 3. T 4. F 5. T

RECALLING DETAILS 1. library, post office, bank, shopping center (any three) 2. large print schedules, audiocassette tapes

USING THE SCHEDULE: 1. 7 2. 41 3. 10 minutes 4. Lee

REASONING: 1. The first bus arrives at school at 7:25. 2. It is a weekday schedule.

ON YOUR OWN: Answers will vary.

Lesson 4: Easy, Economical Rides

THINKING IT OVER: 1. b 2. a 3. a 4. c 5. c 6. b

EVERYDAY MATH: 1. $3.10 2. $62 3. $6

MAKING INFERENCES: 1. Adventure Pass 2. School Pass 3. Quick Tik

ON YOUR OWN: Answers will vary.

Unit 2: Review

A. Answers will vary.

B. 1. allows a rider to switch buses without paying another fare 2. a place where commuters can park their cars and catch a bus 3. an electrically powered train that travels underground 4. a designated area where bus travel is free

C. when buses arrive at scheduled stops; which stops are transfer points; the locations of scheduled stops; what time the last bus of the day leaves your stop

D. Answers will vary.

UNIT 3: TRAVELING BY TRAIN OR PLANE

Lesson 1: The Benefits of Traveling by Train

THINKING IT OVER: 1. a 2. b 3. b 4. c

KEY VOCABULARY: 1. acceleration 2. berths 3. Outskirts 4. skyline

COLORFUL LANGUAGE: 1. feast your eyes 2. bird's-eye view

FACT AND OPINION: 1. O 2. F 3. F 4. O 5. F

ON YOUR OWN: Answers will vary.

Lesson 2: Buying Airline Tickets

THINKING IT OVER: 1. c 2. b 3. c

KEY VOCABULARY: 1. c 2. d 3. a 4. b 5. e 6. g 7. f

EVERYDAY MATH: 1. one-half 2. $100 3. less

MAKING INFERENCES: Answers will vary.

ON YOUR OWN: Answers will vary.

Lesson 3: Reading a Flight Itinerary

THINKING IT OVER: 1. It serves as a purchase receipt and summarizes travel plans. 2. with a credit card 3. 1870 4. three

UNDERSTANDING TERMS: 1. b 2. a 3. a 4. c

FIGURE IT OUT: 1. a 2. a 3. c 4. c 5. a 6. a 7. c

ON YOUR OWN: Answers will vary.

Lesson 4: Overseas Travel

THINKING IT OVER: 1. immunization record, medical history, supply of medications, your doctor's phone number, passport 2. application form, money, photographs, identification, proof of citizenship

KEY VOCABULARY: 1. passport 2. citizen 3. embassy 4. visa 5. immunization

RECALLING DETAILS: 1. $60 2. U.S. embassy 3. travel warnings 4. problems, blood type, medications, doctor's name and phone number 5. reading travel guides, calling agencies, checking Internet sites

ON YOUR OWN: Answers will vary.

Unit 3: Review

A. Answers will vary.

B. 1. the nation's largest passenger rail company   2. a flight that makes at least one stop with no change of planes   3. information about the type of booking   4. medication that protects against a disease

C. Answers will vary.

D. Answers will vary.

UNIT 4: PLANNING A VACATION

Lesson 1: Selecting a Travel Destination

THINKING IT OVER: 1. b   2. c   3. c

KEY VOCABULARY: 1. destination   2. Statistics   3. duffel bag   4. brochure   5. bureau

INFORMAL LANGUAGE: 1. a   2. c

RECALLING DETAILS: 1. bookstores, online, TV   2. crowds, inflated prices, full hotels, busy restaurants

COMPARING AND CONTRASTING: Answers will vary but could include: A vacation cannot be returned if dissatisfied. It can't be tried first like a product can.

ON YOUR OWN: Answers will vary.

Lesson 2: Planning Your Travel Budget

THINKING IT OVER: 1. food, entertainment   2. c, d, e, f, h

KEY VOCABULARY: 1. made a careful guess about it   2. mixed collection   3. peak season   4. serve themselves from a main table   5. kitty

EVERYDAY MATH 1. b   2. a   3. a

PLEASE EXPLAIN: Answers will vary.

ON YOUR OWN: Answers will vary.

Lesson 3: Fly or Drive?

THINKING IT OVER: Answers will vary.

KEY VOCABULARY: 1. Depreciation   2. Tolls   3. Baggage

INFORMAL LANGUAGE: 1. turn up their noses   2. catch some shut-eye   3. time is money

FLY OR DRIVE? 1. D   2. F   3. F   4. D   5. D

EVERYDAY MATH: $241.20

ON YOUR OWN: Answers will vary.

Lesson 4: Choosing a Hotel or Motel: Luxury or Economy?

THINKING IT OVER: 1. a   2. c   3. a   4. b

KEY VOCABULARY: 1. hotel   2. motel   3. valet   4. Amenities   5. Luxurious   6. lobby   7. tip

RECALLING DETAILS: Answers will vary.

ON YOUR OWN: Answers will vary.

Unit 4: Review

A. Answers will vary.

B. 1. a meal in which people serve themselves from a main table   2. a lodging with rooms for rent that is usually one or two stories high   3. provide services for guests, such as caring for clothes or parking cars

C. 1. T   2. F   3. F   4. T   5. T   6. F

D. Answers will vary.

—BOOK 10—
CAR AND DRIVER

UNIT 1: BECOMING A GOOD DRIVER

Lesson 1: Learning to Drive

THINKING IT OVER: 1. c   2. a   3. b   4. a

EVERYDAY MATH: 1. 40   2. 6   3. 34

KEY VOCABULARY: 1. classroom instruction to prepare for the written test for a driver's permit   2. behind-the-wheel instruction and practice   3. someone under 18 years old   4. practice driving with a licensed adult   5. drive on your own

DRAWING CONCLUSIONS: Young people tend to be more careless and are less experienced.

ON YOUR OWN: Answers will vary.

Lesson 2: Driver's License

THINKING IT OVER: 1. T   2. F   3. F   4. T

EVERYDAY MATH: 1. $272   2. $3,600; $300

KEY VOCABULARY: 1. a marked or unmarked area for pedestrians to cross the street   2. stops the car   3. go faster

RECALLING DETAILS: 1. c   2. a   3. b

ON YOUR OWN: Students should mention that a driver needs to check traffic flow, signal, time his or her entry onto the freeway, check over shoulder when accelerating into gap in traffic, signal early and slow down on the exit ramp to the posted speed limit, and adjust speed to road conditions.

Lesson 3: Bad Weather and Other Hazards

THINKING IT OVER: 1. 400 feet   2. weather and road conditions   3. low beams   4. pull completely off the road   5. 30 mph

EVERYDAY MATH: 4

KEY VOCABULARY: 1. to respond in some way 2. miles per hour   3. put it off for a time 4. make it bigger   5. slight rain

CAUSE AND EFFECT: 1. so you can stop quickly if necessary   2. the light will reflect back and cause glare

ON YOUR OWN: Sample answer: When driving near a playground, slow down so you can stop quickly in case a child runs out in front of you.

Lesson 4: Using a City Map

THINKING IT OVER: 1. c   2. a   3. c   4. a

EVERYDAY MATH: 1. $38   2. $7.50, $57.50

KEY VOCABULARY: 1. an image on a map that identifies north, south, west, and east 2. the section location of streets, parks, etc.   3. water

PUTTING DETAILS IN ORDER: 4, 1, 2, 3

ON YOUR OWN: Answers will vary.

Unit 1: Review

A. 1. b   2. a   3. b   4. a

B. 1. compass rose   2. driver's license 3. driver education

C. 1. adjust the mirrors and fasten safety belt   2. I would slow down.   3. review the appropriate section in the driver handbook

UNIT 2: BUYING A CAR

Lesson 1: Sticking to Your Budget

THINKING IT OVER: 1. c   2. a   3. b   4. c

KEY VOCABULARY: 1. Manufacturer's Suggested Retail Price   2. the same as the MSRP 3. the price the dealer probably paid   4. can bargain   5. the difference between the price the dealer pays and the price he gets

EVERYDAY MATH: 1. $3,145   2. $15,815.65

ON YOUR OWN: Answers will vary. (Negotiate with the salesperson.)

Lesson 2: Comparing Used Cars

THINKING IT OVER: 1. F   2. F   3. T   4. T

EVERYDAY MATH: 1. $3,400   2. 20,000 3. $14,400

KEY VOCABULARY: 1. a guarantee   2. looked over, examined   3. how many miles the car goes on a gallon of gas   4. repairs cars and performs routine maintenance

COMPARING: 1. c   2. c

ON YOUR OWN: Possible answer: a used car, because a new car would be too expensive

Lesson 3: Interpreting a New Car Sticker

THINKING IT OVER: 1. the engine   2. add to the price of the car   3. does   4. makes even more profit if you use their financing 5. wants to downplay the real cost of the car

EVERYDAY MATH: 1. $2,808   2. 111

KEY VOCABULARY: 1. four-wheel drive   2. vehicle identification number   3. extra   4. careful 5. choices

SUMMARIZING: Answers will vary.

ON YOUR OWN: Answers will vary.

Lesson 4: Financing a Car

THINKING IT OVER: 1. cash   2. get preapproved before you shop   3. you deduct the interest from your income, reducing your taxes 4. the interest rate is often lower than that at a bank

EVERYDAY MATH: 1. $1,700   2. $7,500

KEY VOCABULARY: 1. money   2. annual percentage rate   3. the difference between what you owe and what the home is worth 4. find out how much you can get before you shop   5. the extra you'll pay for the money

DRAWING CONCLUSIONS: 1. a   2. b

ON YOUR OWN: Possible answer: Sell the car and get a cheaper one.

Unit 2: Review

A. 1. b   2. a   3. c   4. a

B. 1. down payment   2. sticker price; MSRP   3. the dealer's profit

C. 1. Determine what you can pay, shop

around for a loan with a good rate, get preapproved.   2. negotiate for a better price   3. Possible answer: complain about how you are being treated and insist on seeing the car that's advertised

UNIT 3: MAINTENANCE AND REPAIR

Lesson 1: Benefits of Upkeep

THINKING IT OVER: 1. c   2. a   3. b   4. b

EVERYDAY MATH: 1. $15.75   2. 6

KEY VOCABULARY: 1. expensive   2. works well   3. liquids   4. necessary   5. correct

SUMMARIZING: You should take care of your car to avoid costly repair bills and to keep your car safe.

ON YOUR OWN: Sample answers: Check the hoses and their connections to avoid leaks. Check the wires to make sure they're secure. Check the battery terminals for corrosion. Check the lights to make sure they're working.

Lesson 2: Car Repair Estimates

THINKING IT OVER: 1. F   2. T   3. F   4. F   5. T

EVERYDAY MATH: 1. $767; $2,825.33   2. $300; $654

KEY VOCABULARY: 1. a good guess   2. a small amount of damage   3. the money you have to pay before the insurance company will pay a bill   4. demands made by a policy holder against an insurance company

DRAWING CONCLUSIONS: b

ON YOUR OWN: Sample answer: I'd take the policy with the $500 deductible because I'm a very careful driver and I've never had an accident. I'd rather take my chances than pay the higher premiums.

Lesson 3: Instructions for Using Jumper Cables

THINKING IT OVER: 1. it will drain your battery   2. to avoid shock   3. the car with the dead battery won't start on its own   4. for safety's sake

EVERYDAY MATH: 1. 60   2. 52

KEY VOCABULARY : 1. use another car's battery to start it   2. turn the key that stops the engine   3. an enclosed area   4. unplug them

PUTTING DETAILS IN ORDER: 3, 4, 2, 7, 5, 6, 1

ON YOUR OWN: Some items could be jumper cables, flashlight, flares, spare tire, jack, drinking water, empty gas can, rags, blanket, quart of oil, funnel for oil, first aid kit, paper towels, a wrench, a pair of pliers

Lesson 4: New Tire Warranty

THINKING IT OVER: 1. pay a fee   2. the tread is down to 3/32 of an inch   3. cannot   4. for tire balancing

EVERYDAY MATH: $385

KEY VOCABULARY: 1. first   2. money back   3. buyer   4. substitute   5. harmed   6. needed   7. like   8. what you think   9. crash

DRAWING CONCLUSIONS: 1. Yes. It was a normal road hazard.   2. No. The uneven wear was his own fault because his car had a mechanical defect.

ON YOUR OWN: Sample answer: Check tire pressure regularly; make sure car is aligned properly; rotate tires regularly.

Unit 3: Review

A.   1. b   2. a   3. b   4. c

B.   1. air filter   2. deductible   3. jumper cables

C.   1. get a jump start   2. get three estimates, evaluate the estimates, contact the insurance company, get the repairs done   3. get a new battery

UNIT 4: DRIVING AND THE LAW

Lesson 1: Automobile Registration

THINKING IT OVER: 1. the dealer gets the car registered for you   2. you must register the car within 10 days   3. within six to eight weeks   4. within five days

EVERYDAY MATH: 1. $142   2. $113.60   3. $85.20   4. $104

KEY VOCABULARY: 1. buy   2. turn in   3. papers

SUMMARIZING: The dealer collects the sales tax and fees from you. The dealer submits the fees and documents to the DMV.

ON YOUR OWN: Any two: so you can be traced if the car is used during a crime; so the state can collect taxes to keep the roads maintained; so the state can keep track of your compliance with smog laws

Lesson 2: Shopping for Car Insurance

THINKING IT OVER: 1. F   2. T   3. T   4. F   5. F

EVERYDAY MATH: 1. $672   2. $13.20

KEY VOCABULARY: 1. insurance that protects you in case of theft, fire, or damage to your car 2. the money that comes out of your pocket when you file a claim   3. the amount you pay for insurance   4. money off

RECALLING DETAILS: Any three: shop around; get a higher deductible; take a driver training course; earn good grades; have a good driving record; get airbags; get a car alarm

ON YOUR OWN: Sample answer: Yes. I'd get them to protect my investment and for peace of mind.

Lesson 3: Traffic and Parking Tickets

THINKING IT OVER: 1. appear in traffic court 2. pay bail   3. made a guilty plea 4. tell the DMV   5. 8 points in 36 months 6. 3 years

EVERYDAY MATH: 1. $42\frac{1}{2}$ hours   2. $\frac{1}{3}$ point; $\frac{1}{4}$ point; .22 point

KEY VOCABULARY: 1. written up with a ticket 2. pay no attention to   3. tell, inform 4. a guilty verdict   5. avoiding, running away from

CAUSE AND EFFECT: driving under the influence of alcohol or drugs; driving while judgment is impaired by too many drinks or medication; hit-and-run driving that causes an accident and leaving the scene

ON YOUR OWN: Answers will vary.

Lesson 4: Drinking and Driving

THINKING IT OVER: 1. more   2. definitely 3. probably   4. is

EVERYDAY MATH: 1. 6   2. 4

KEY VOCABULARY: 1. against the law   2. one that is used for business purposes   3. many, several, a variety   4. for sure, certain

EXTEND THE LESSON: Sample answer: Choose a "designated driver" who will not drink any alcohol and will do all the driving.

ON YOUR OWN: Sample answer: I would drive myself there and back. I would make sure that someone who drank too much did not get in a car and drive.

Unit 4: Review

A.   1. b   2. c   3. a   4. b

B.   1. comprehensive   2. ticket

C.   1. a bad thing because they indicate that you've done dangerous or illegal things while driving   2. protest the ticket and explain to the judge that the meter is not accurate   3. Sample answer: pay for the entire bill and not get the insurance company involved 4. Sample answer: I'd get the keys from my friend, and I'd do the driving, or I'd call a cab.

—BOOK 1—
MOVING OUT ON YOUR OWN

UNIT 1: READINESS FOR INDEPENDENCE

KEY WORDS IN CONTEXT:

A.
```
    D E C R E A S E
      C A L E N D A R T
    A   H         Y   N
  C T   A       C   E
  S I   T B D   N   D
  Y N T   I E       N
  S C   C T T   B   E
  T O     E U T   P
  E M   P H D       E
  M E M       E   D
  X O E G D E L W O N K N
    C R I T I C I S M     I
```

B. 1. hectic 2. decrease, debt
3. competency 4. calendar, system
5. knowledge, independent
6. attitude, habit

UNIT 2: FINDING AN APARTMENT

SYNONYMS AND ANTONYMS:

A. ACROSS: 2. pros 4. vacant 6. rent
7. present
DOWN: 1. essential 2. prevent
3. decorate 5. allowed

B. 1. previous 2. identify 3. proposed
4. authorized 5. tenant 6. features
7. amount

UNIT 3: MOVING IN AND GETTING SETTLED

WHAT IS IT?

A. 1. telephone 2. post office
3. landlord 4. individual 5. relatives
6. secondhand 7. lease 8. trailer

B. ACROSS: 1. desk 4. hitch 6. van
7. cable
DOWN: 2. electricity 3. linens 5. address

UNIT 4: SOLVING COMMON PROBLEMS

FACT OR OPINION?

A. 1. O 2. O 3. F 4. O 5. F 6. F

B. Answers will vary, but could include:
1. keep the place clean 2. entertainment
3. hang outdoor clotheslines; have pets
4. spend carefully, save, etc.

UNITS 1–4: COMPREHENSION

1. b 2. c 3. c 4. b 5. a 6. b 7. c

UNITS 1–4: DICTIONARY DRILL

A. Answers will vary.

B. 1. noun, 2, second 2. noun, 5, second
3. noun, 4, first 4. verb, 3, first

—BOOK 2—
EVERYDAY HOUSEHOLD TASKS

UNIT 1: GROCERY SHOPPING

KEY WORDS IN CONTEXT:

A.
```
      S E A S O N A L E
          I           S
  S       A       T   W
  E P   G R A I N   O
  R   R     E       R
  V   A O       I   B
  I B     D   S P
  N I     E   U A
  G N   R   N C N
    S G S E L P A T S
    N   M       R S
  I R I G I D       Y
```

B. 1. products, staples 2. browse, bins
3. grain 4. menus, rigid
5. Seasonal 6. pantry 7. serving

UNIT 2: COOKING

SYNONYMS AND ANTONYMS:

A. ACROSS: 2. recipe 4. appetizers
7. techniques 8. canister
DOWN: 1. spices 2. tips 5. portions
6. terms

B. 1. flexible, c 2. cooked, a
3. soak, e 4. thaw, f 5. boiling, b
6. rarely, d

UNIT 3: CARING FOR YOUR CLOTHES

WHAT IS IT?

A. 1. synthetics 2. detergent
3. garment 4. stains 5. steam iron
6. care label 7. wooden hangers
8. bleach

B. 1. chlorine 2. cool or cold 3. knit
4. plastic 5. sachet

UNIT 4: HOME MAINTENANCE AND DECORATING

RECALLING DETAILS:

A. 1. c 2. c 3. c 4. b 5. c 6. b

B. 1. F 2. T 3. F 4. F 5. F 6. T

UNITS 1–4: COMPREHENSION

A. 1. F 2. F 3. T 4. T 5. T
6. F 7. T

B. Kinds of Fabric: cotton, synthetics, blends – wool
Cooking Methods: simmer, parboil, bake – stir-fry
Dairy Products: yogurt, milk, cheese – ice cream
Home Appliances: washer, vacuum, crockpot – toaster

UNITS 1–4: DICTIONARY DRILLS

1. something that is produced, esp. fruits and vegetables marketed in stores; to bring forth, bear, yield, make or manufacture something 2. to cook in water that is just below the boiling point or in a small cup put over boiling water; to hunt or catch fish or game on another person's property without being allowed to do so 3. to cut something such as potatoes into small cubes; small cubes, used in games, that are marked on each side with a different number of dots ranging from one to six 4. any article of food or other common item that is regularly used and kept in large amounts; U-shaped piece of wire with sharp pointed ends that is driven through papers or other materials to fasten them together 5. a chest of drawers for holding clothes; an agency that provides certain kinds of information or services or a department of the government

—BOOK 3—
HEALTH AND SAFETY

UNIT 1: PREVENTION: THE BEST CURE

KEY WORDS IN CONTEXT:

A.
```
      T N E I D E R G N I
S E I R O L A C       U
C A L C I U M     S   T
D             N   N E
C A         I     E N
I G N       H I N S
B E   D   P   R E   I
O R   R   O   U   Y L
R M   O   U     Y   S
E S D   N F     X
A N           F L O S S
E S A E R G
```

B. 1. calories 2. dandruff 3. Aerobic, oxygen 4. utensils, germs 5. floss 6. grease 7. Calcium 8. Endorphins

UNIT 2: GETTING MEDICAL ATTENTION

SYNONYMS AND ANTONYMS:

A. 1. cleaning 2. heartbeat 3. emotions 4. counselor 5. tension 6. payments 7. remove 8. injury 9. regular 10. subscribe

B. 1. c 2. f 3. e 4. a 5. d 6. b

UNIT 3: HANDLING HEALTH PROBLEMS

WHAT IS IT?

A. 1. allergy 2. first aid 3. diarrhea 4. dosage 5. dizziness 6. side effect 7. depression 8. emergency

B. 1. Generic 2. moles 3. tablet 4. bruise 5. antiseptics

UNIT 4: AVOIDING HEALTH HAZARDS

CAUSE AND EFFECT:

A. 1. c 2. e 3. g. 4. f 5. d 6. b 7. h 8. a

B. 1. Answers will vary. 2. quitting smoking 3. Drinking, driving 4. tobacco 5. STDs, sexually transmitted diseases

UNITS 1–4: COMPREHENSION

A. 1. O 2. F 3. F 4. O 5. O 6. F

B. 1. price 2. penicillin 3. alcoholism 4. cheese 5. weightlifting

UNITS 1–4: DICTIONARY DRILL

A. ACROSS: 3. technical 5. infectious
6. medical 7. sugary
DOWN: 1. nutritious 2. allergic
4. hygienic

B. antihistamine, vegetable, deductible,
hepatitis, antiseptic, temperature
1.–6. Sentences will vary.

—BOOK 4—
MANAGING MONEY

UNIT 1: CONTROLLING YOUR SPENDING

KEY WORDS IN CONTEXT:

A.
```
E T A D P U
S   E     F I N E S D
T   M     M       E
A       P F R U G A L
T   U   T R M     A
E   L   A U   I   I
M S     H T M   C
E     C     I   N
N   R       N O A
T N E M U C O D I   N
X V D R O C E R M   I
O R E G I S T E R   F
```

B. 1. temptation 2. frugal 3. statement
4. update, register 5. financial, record
6. impulse 7. overcharged

UNIT 2: BANKING BASICS

SYNONYMS AND ANTONYMS:

A. ACROSS: 1. funds 2. annual
4. expenses
DOWN: 1. fines 2. amount 3. fees

B. 1. avoid, f 2. multiply, d
3. deposit, e 4. fixed, b
5. add, a 6. saving, c

UNIT 3: BUY NOW, PAY LATER

WHAT IS IT?

A. 1. annual percentage rate
2. installment 3. investment
4. grace period 5. principal
6. application 7. refund
8. loan

B. 1. Internet 2. finance charge
3. borrower 4. rent-to-own
5. co-signer 6. cards

UNIT 4: IMPROVING YOUR BUDGETING SKILLS

IDENTIFYING MAIN IDEAS:

A. 1. T 2. F 3. F 4. T 5. T 6. F
7. T 8. T

B. 1. b 2. c 3. a

UNITS 1–4: COMPREHENSION

1. You use a deposit slip to put money
in the bank and a withdrawal slip to
take money out. 2. Answers will vary.
3. bounced check 4. keep you from
getting a loan, place to live, job, etc.
5. Interest charges raise the balance.
6. the final payment on an installment
purchase that's much larger than the
payments you've been making
7. Answers will vary, but should include
food, clothes, etc.; rent, loan payment,
etc. 8. have a credit card; have
savings in the bank

UNITS 1–4: DICTIONARY DRILL

2. affordable 3. exceed 4. pay
5. accomplishment 6. management
7. expensive 8. transact 9. risky
Sentences will vary.

—BOOK 5—
CONSUMER SPENDING

UNIT 1: THE WISE BUYER

KEY WORDS IN CONTEXT:

A.
```
    O   R A A Z A B   S
    V   F D O N A T E D
    E   I       V E
  B R A N D X   I   T
  R S         T   O A
  E T         A U   T
  M   A       R T   R S
  U   T   A F L A W   E
  S   E P   E       S
  N M   T N U O C S I D
  O O
  C O N S I G N M E N T
```

B. 1. discount 2. comparatives
3. brand 4. overstate 5. bazaar,
donated 6. flaw, outlet 7. fixtures 8.
estate

UNIT 2: SHOPPING FOR GOODS

SYNONYMS AND ANTONYMS:

A. ACROSS: 3. assistant   4. merchandise
5. features   7. policy
DOWN: 1. warranty   2. style   5. fabric
6. repair

B. 1. permanent, b   2. avoid, d
3. arrives, e   4. defective, f
5. used, c   6. cheap, a

UNIT 3: SHOPPING FOR SERVICES

WHAT IS IT?

A. 1. reputation   2. estimate   3. mechanic
4. references   5. premiums   6. caution

B. 1. warning   2. guarantee   3. policy
4. warranty   5. license   6. labor
7. beneficiary

UNIT 4: CONSUMER RIGHTS

TRUE OR FALSE?

1. F   2. T   3. T   4. T   5. T   6. F
7. F   8. T   9. F   10. T   11. T   12. T

UNITS 1–4: COMPREHENSION

1. c   2. a   3. a   4. b   5. d   6. d

UNITS 1–4: DICTIONARY DRILL

1. different, principle   2. particular,
resistant   3. opinion, exaggerate
4. labels, similar   5. merchandise,
receipt   6. interpret, warranty
7. professional services
8. recommend, guarantee

—BOOK 6—
JOB SEARCH

UNIT 1: WORKPLACE READINESS

KEY WORDS IN CONTEXT:

A.
```
    Y T I N U T R O P P O
  F A           T
    E   P   B R           C
A H     P A E L           U
    C   L I R A N         R
      A N   C E   E       R
    O I D I       N F     E
  G N   R E         T   I N
  G   E     M       R I T
    L         Y A C       T
  C   E C N A V D A E
  P E N S I O N       E
```

UNIT 2: OCCUPATIONAL TRAINING

SYNONYMS AND ANTONYMS:

A. ACROSS: 4. classes   5. percentage
7. customer   8. terminology
DOWN: 1. abilities   2. depend
3. perhaps   6. steady

B. 1. d   2. c   3. b   4. a

C. 1. equal   2. student   3. a necessary
4. Eager

UNIT 3: APPLYING FOR A JOB

WHAT IS IT?

A. 1. agencies   2. abbreviations
3. application   4. manual labor
5. documents   6. computers

B. 1. training, d   2. custodian, e
3. lifeguard, a   4. misdemeanor, c
5. multi-task, b   6. permission, g
7. Internet, f

UNIT 4: THE JOB INTERVIEW

RECALLING DETAILS:

1. talk   2. notice   3. record
4. response   5. spots   6. Calm
7. complement   8. reference
9. conclusion   10. position
11. documents

UNITS 1–4: COMPREHENSION

1. c   2. b   3. d   4. d   5. b   6. d

UNITS 1–4: DICTIONARY DRILL

A. 1. pronunciation   2. failure
3. communication   4. thought
5. selection   6. choice
7. cleanliness   8. information
9. impressive   10. employable
11. written   12. conclusive
13. considerate   14. informative
15. thankful   16. questionable

B. Answers will vary.

C. 1. complementary   2. limousine

—BOOK 7—
GETTING AHEAD AT WORK

UNIT 1: OFF TO A GOOD START

KEY WORDS IN CONTEXT:

A.
```
E T A I R P O R P P A
T D R E S S Y     W
P C C   N   N I N
A   R   O   O   T O
T Y   I I I     H I
N   R   T     H S
O     O U A I     E S
D C     A L U   C L E
U   C   L     I D R
    E   I M A G E   S P
    R   S   V       M
P I S S O G E       I
```

B. 1. evaluations 2. criticism
   3. dressy 4. contact, impression
   5. payroll, withheld 6. dues

UNIT 2: LEARNING THE JOB

SYNONYMS AND ANTONYMS:

A. **ACROSS:** 1. objective 4. verbal
   6. pace 7. discussion
   DOWN: 2. educate 3. employee
   4. valued 5. request

B. 1. fired 2. clarification
   3. complicated 4. beforehand
   5. consistently 6. frequently
   7. positive 8. enthusiasm
   9. genuine 10. prompt

UNIT 3: SUCCEEDING ON THE JOB

WHAT IS IT?

A. 1. progress 2. overtime
   3. appointment 4. competence
   5. standards 6. accuracy

B. 1. output 2. practice, perfect
   3. errors 4. Measure, once
   5. benchmarks 6. trainee

UNIT 4: WORKPLACE PROBLEMS AND SOLUTIONS

TRUE OR FALSE?

1. T 2. F 3. F 4. F 5. T 6. F
7. T 8. T 9. F 10. F 11. T

UNITS 1–4: COMPREHENSION

1. d 2. b 3. a 4. d 5. d 6. c

UNITS 1–4: DICTIONARY DRILL

A. **ACROSS:** 2. initiate 3. satisfy
   4. employ 5. negotiate
   DOWN: 1. rely 3. succeed 4. enter

B. 1. harassment, grievance
   2. occurs, companies 3. dues, salary
   4. foreman's, clarification

—BOOK 8—
COMMUNITY RESOURCES

UNIT 1: YOUR TAXES AT WORK

KEY WORDS IN CONTEXT:

A.
```
C O N F I R M A T I O N
C R   S E R V I C E S
L E   N       I
I C R T A X Y   T   Y
N R   T   T     I   R
C I E   I   I   Z   A
I C A   R   F   O E   R
L   T O     I   N   B
B   I         E S A I
U R O         D   L
P   N I A T N I A M
```

B. 1. Certified, confirmation 2. Public, citizens 3. Priority 4. tax, maintain
   5. national 6. services, clinic
   7. Recreation

UNIT 2: EMERGENCY ASSISTANCE

SYNONYMS AND ANTONYMS:

A. **ACROSS:** 2. inspect 4. pedestrians
   7. attorney 8. security
   DOWN: 1. fees 3. trained 4. preserve
   5. donations 6. goal

B. 1. accidental 2. discourage 3. guilty
   4. defender 5. eventual 6. free
   7. rapidly 8. rural 9. include
   10. shallow

UNIT 3: SERVICES FOR WORKERS

WHAT IS IT?

A. 1. Social Security card
   2. Occupational 3. employment
   4. payroll taxes 5. benefits
   6. Placement 7. Labor
   8. Compensation

B. 1. disposal 2. inspector 3. agency
   4. federal 5. eligible 6. an application

UNIT 4: SERVICES FOR CITIZENS

RECALLING DETAILS:

1. b   2. c   3. d   4. b   5. a   6. c

UNITS 1–4: COMPREHENSION

A. 1. T   2. F   3. F   4. T   5. F   6. F
7. T   8. T

B. 1. d   2. a   3. c   4. b   5. f   6. e

UNITS 1–4: DICTIONARY DRILL

A. ACROSS: 1. assist   4. participate
6. enforce   7. apply   8. elect
DOWN: 2. transport   3. regulate
5. refer

B. 1. some benefit or advantage desired by an individual or a group; money paid for the use of someone else's money
2. to manage, control, take care of; part by which something can be held or lifted with the hand
3. the act of observing or guarding; a device for telling time that looks like a small clock   4. the special duty a government group is sent out to perform; the place where religious missionaries live and work

---

—BOOK 9—
PUBLIC TRANSPORTATION
AND TRAVEL

UNIT 1: COMMUTING TO SCHOOL AND WORK

KEY WORDS IN CONTEXT:

A.
```
    B   E V I S N E F E D
  S   E K I H H C T I H S
  R   N S T R O L L   T
  C E   E       A S   R
  A   T   F   C   T S E
    R   U   I E   R T N
  T   P   M   T   A S U
    A   O   M U S N I O
    N   O   O   G L U
    O   D   L R C E C S
    C       E       R Y
  E           M       C
```

B. 1. commuters, stroll   2. carpool, economical   3. tandem, cyclists
4. benefits, strenuous   5. hitchhike, stranger   6. route   7. Defensive

---

UNIT 2: TRAVELING BY BUS

SYNONYMS AND ANTONYMS:

A. ACROSS: 2. tracks   5. passenger
6. fleet   8. costly
DOWN: 1. motorist   3. schedule
4. fare   7. tips

B. 1. common   2. urban   3. arrive
4. subway   5. allows   6. regular

UNIT 3: TRAVELING BY TRAIN OR PLANE

WHAT IS IT?

A. 1. itinerary   2. departure
3. compartment   4. slogan
5. Amtrak   6. passport

B. 1. reservation   2. overseas
3. confirmation   4. restrictions
5. application   6. immunization
7. refund   8. visa

UNIT 4: PLANNING A VACATION

DRAWING CONCLUSIONS:

1. b   2. d   3. a   4. c   5. b   6. b

UNITS 1–4: COMPREHENSION

A. 1. Hitchhiking   2. accessible to
3. lung   4. vehicle   5. lanes
6. transportation   7. A legend
8. detour

B. 1. There are fewer passengers because people are not going to and from work.   2. They will avoid boredom and the temptation to quit walking if they get some variety.

UNITS 1–4: DICTIONARY DRILL

A. 1. beneficial   2. decency   3. optional
4. scenic   5. economy   6. moderation
7. environmental   8. enthusiasm
9. distant   10. protective

B. 1. hitchhiker   2. accommodations
3. accessible   4. libraries
5. passengers   6. itinerary
7. immunizations   8. brochure

—BOOK 10—
CAR AND DRIVER

UNIT 1: BECOMING A GOOD DRIVER

KEY WORDS IN CONTEXT:

A.
```
        T R A F F I C   D S
                    L     U
      D   M       E       P
        E   I     I       E
        F   N Y K   G     R
      G E A R   O   N     V
        X   O R     I     I
      D   E B S     N     S
      I     D     T   I   E
      L N N         E A   D
      A   I     T I M R E P
      H V L I C E N S E T
```

B. 1. index   2. training   3. minor
4. defroster   5. yield   6. handbook
7. traffic

UNIT 2: BUYING A CAR

SYNONYMS AND ANTONYMS:

A. 1. guarantee   2. repairman
3. recommended   4. label   5. add-ons
6. examine   7. worth   8. gasoline
9. upkeep   10. preowned

B. 1. negotiable   2. borrow   3. wholesale
4. profit   5. thorough   6. average
7. add

UNIT 3: MAINTENANCE AND REPAIR

WHAT IS IT?

A. 1. d   2. e   3. b   4. f   5. a   6. c   7. g

B. 1. oil   2. air filter   3. air pressure
4. battery   5. engine   6. headlights

UNIT 4: DRIVING AND THE LAW

RECALLING DETAILS:

1. a   2. c   3. c   4. a   5. b   6. a   7. c

UNITS 1–4: COMPREHENSION

A. Parts of a Car: headlights, battery, heater, engine
Parts of a Map: index, compass rose, legend, symbols
Road Hazards: fog, playground, drizzle, construction
Car Insurance: liability, collision, coverage, deductible
Heading: Answers will vary, but should suggest "driving mistakes."

B. 1. dealer   2. neutral   3. ramp
4. signals   5. lanes   6. pedal

UNITS 1–4: DICTIONARY DRILL

1. 4, a device that shows or measures the speed of a revolving shaft   2. 3, arrangement in a straight line; the condition of being able to work well together   3. 3, moving out or lying in the same direction and always the same distance apart so as to never meet   4. 4, an electric generator that produces alternating current
5. 3, the legal right to move in front of others at an intersection, etc.
6. 1, to order someone to appear in a court of law   7. 2, to give up or lose something because of a mistake or failure to do something

NAME _____

DATE _____

KEY WORDS IN CONTEXT

A. Circle the hidden words. They may go up, down, across, backward, or diagonally. Check off each word as you find it.

___ **KNOWLEDGE**	___ **DEBT**
___ **ATTITUDE**	___ **HECTIC**
___ **COMPETENCY**	___ **HABIT**
___ **CALENDAR**	___ **INCOME**
___ **DECREASE**	___ **SYSTEM**
___ **INDEPENDENT**	___ **CRITICISM**

```
B D E C R E A S E S E W
N P Q C A L E N D A R T
O A D F H X C H J Y O N
C W T E A S T Y C L K E
S I M T B D O N P H I D
Y N T Q I Z E K R T G N
S C E C T A B J D C E
T O S A E S U E T A M P
E M D P G H S D O L B E
M E M F C P A G E F R D
X O E G D E L W O N K N
C R I T I C I S M I Y I
```

B. Use puzzle words to correctly complete the sentences.

1. If you've scheduled too many things to do, you will have a _____ day.

2. To _____ your _____, make extra payments on your credit card bill.

3. A _____ is a task you know how to do well, such as mowing and edging the lawn.

4. Marking appointments on a _____ is a good _____ of time management.

5. Do you have the skills and _____ you need to become an _____ adult?

6. Over time, a bad _____ becomes a thinking _____.

NAME _____

DATE _____

SYNONYMS AND ANTONYMS

A. Complete the crossword puzzle with words from Unit 2.
Answer words are *antonyms* (words with opposite meanings) of the clue words.

ACROSS

2. cons
4. occupied
6. own
7. past

DOWN

1. unnecessary
2. permit
3. strip
5. prohibited

(crossword grid with letters: 1 E, 2 P, 3 D, 4 V, 5 A, 6 R, 7 P)

B. Find a *synonym* (word with a similar meaning) in the box for each **boldface** word. Write the synonym on the line.

landlord	current	previous	forbidden	proposed
features	tenant	engaged	customer	authorized
official	guest	amount	manager	identify

1. Write your **former** _____ address on the rental application.

2. Please **name** _____ the owner of your apartment building.

3. What is your "**suggested** _____ date of occupancy"?

4. Who have you **allowed** _____ to obtain a copy of your credit report?

5. Bill has been a **renter** _____ in that building for two years.

6. Anne's new apartment has many attractive **characteristics** _____ .

7. Your income is the total **sum** _____ of money you receive on a regular basis.

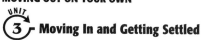

NAME _____

DATE _____

WHAT IS IT?

A. Unscramble the words to complete the sentences.

1. Eduardo needed **LETNEEPOH** _____ service in order to hook up to the Internet.

2. Nick picked up a change of address form at the **STOP COFIEF** _____ _____.

3. Water is the only utility the **DORLNALD** _____ usually pays for.

4. If just one person is moving, check **DUALIDIVIN** _____ on the change of address form.

5. Your **STIVELEAR** _____ may be willing to give you some used furniture.

6. Goodwill and Salvation Army stores offer **DESCONDANH** _____ furniture at low prices.

7. A **ESALE** _____ is a rental contract, usually for a term of one year.

8. If you don't own very much, you can rent a **RATRILE** _____ to move to your new place.

B. Use the clues to help you complete the crossword puzzle with words from the unit.

ACROSS

1. can be made of a flat door and two filing cabinets
4. You need this on your car to pull a trailer.
6. big truck that can haul a houseful of furniture
7. hook-up that provides many TV channels

DOWN

2. utility that provides light
3. sheets, towels, etc.
5. name of your street, number of your house

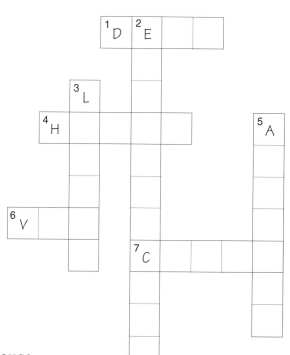

FACT OR OPINION?

A. Write **F** for *fact* or **O** for *opinion* next to each statement.

1. _____ Light blue is the most restful color to paint bedroom walls.

2. _____ All roommates should try to eat about the same amount of food.

3. _____ Apartment managers usually forbid noisy parties and loud music.

4. _____ One good way to prepare for unexpected expenses is to save change in a big jar.

5. _____ A landlord is legally obliged to keep plumbing and heating equipment in good repair.

6. _____ Equal sharing of household chores usually helps roommates get along better.

B. Complete each statement, making it either a *fact* or an *opinion*, as designated.

1. **FACT:** After moving in, it is your responsibility to _____

_____.

2. **OPINION:** When revising your budget, the easiest item to cut is

_____.

3. **FACT:** Two things a landlord might forbid tenants to do are

_____

and _____.

4. **OPINION:** The best way to avoid falling into debt is _____

_____.

COMPREHENSION

Circle a letter to answer the question or complete the sentence.

1. **If you don't count on anyone else for money to live on, you are**

   a. politically independent.

   b. financially independent.

   c. emotionally independent.

2. **Bad attitudes are**

   a. expressed in our behavior.

   b. harmful thinking habits.

   c. both a. and b.

3. **Competent people make the effort to budget their**

   a. wants and needs.

   b. nickels and dimes.

   c. time and money.

4. **Why is your take-home pay less than your salary?**

   a. The payroll clerk takes a fee.

   b. Taxes have been withheld.

   c. Someone is cheating you.

5. **A one-room apartment containing a kitchenette and a bathroom is a**

   a. studio.

   b. condo.

   c. townhouse.

6. **Two good credit references would be**

   a. your teacher and your hairdresser.

   b. your bank and your credit card company.

   c. your grandmother and your uncle.

7. **If you have gas and electricity turned on before you move,**

   a. you'll have to pay a bigger deposit.

   b. the previous tenant will benefit.

   c. your service will be uninterrupted.

DICTIONARY DRILL

A. *Multiple-meaning* words have entirely different meanings when they're used in different contexts. The word *bow*, for example, can mean to bend at the waist or the weapon that shoots arrows. Look up each **boldface** word in the dictionary. Then write an original sentence in which the word has a different meaning.

1. **stick** to a budget _____

_____

2. lucky **breaks** _____

_____

3. to **fall** behind _____

_____

4. keep **track** of _____

_____

5. **pro** and con _____

_____

B. Look up the following words. Use information in the entry to answer the questions.

1. **success**   part of speech? _____ number of syllables? _____

accent on which syllable? _____

2. **abbreviation**   part of speech? _____ number of syllables? _____

accent on which syllable? _____

3. **competency**   part of speech? _____ number of syllables? _____

accent on which syllable? _____

4. **authorize**   part of speech? _____ number of syllables? _____

accent on which syllable? _____

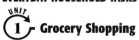
KEY WORDS IN CONTEXT

A. Circle the hidden words. They may go up, down, across, backward, or diagonally. Check off each word as you find it.

___ **PRODUCTS**   ___ **GRAIN**

___ **BARGAIN**   ___ **BINS**

___ **STAPLES**   ___ **MENUS**

___ **SERVING**   ___ **RIGID**

___ **SEASONAL**   ___ **PANTRY**

___ **INGREDIENTS**   ___ **BROWSE**

D	P	S	E	A	S	O	N	A	L	E
L	B	K	J	S	X	I	E	W	Q	S
S	N	E	C	B	A	M	L	O	T	W
E	V	P	A	G	R	A	I	N	W	O
R	E	S	R	D	H	Y	E	U	C	R
V	O	A	F	O	S	I	O	N	L	B
I	B	L	K	A	D	P	S	P	E	S
N	I	V	C	E	S	U	O	A	L	N
G	N	E	R	S	N	F	C	N	E	A
A	S	G	S	E	L	P	A	T	S	L
Z	N	O	M	L	G	H	K	R	S	R
I	R	I	G	I	D	O	P	Y	Y	H

B. Add the correct puzzle word to complete each sentence below.

1. Food _____ such as flour, sugar, bread, and milk are called grocery _____.

2. When you shop, _____ the produce _____ for the best-looking fruits and vegetables.

3. Eat 6 to 11 daily servings from the _____ products group.

4. Plan _____ for the week, but don't be too _____ in making substitutions.

5. _____ foods are best at only certain times of the year.

6. Three places to store food are the refrigerator, freezer, and _____.

7. A single slice of bread counts as one _____ from the grain products group.

SYNONYMS AND ANTONYMS

A. Complete the crossword puzzle with words from the box. Answers words are *synonyms* (words with the same or almost the same meaning) of the clue words. Hint: You will *not* use all the words in the box.

| ingredients | terms | canister | spices | appetizers |
| techniques | tips | utensil | recipe | portions |

ACROSS

2. formula

4. hors d'oeuvres

7. procedures

8. container

DOWN

1. seasonings

2. hints

5. servings

6. words

B. You know that *antonyms* are words with opposite meanings. First, unscramble the **boldface** words from the unit Then, write a letter to match each unscrambled word with its antonym.

1. _____ **BLEXILEF** _____   a. raw

2. _____ **DOKEOC** _____   b. cooling

3. _____ **OAKS** _____   c. stiff

4. _____ **WHAT** _____   d. frequently

5. _____ **NIGLOIB** _____   e. drain

6. _____ **REYRAL** _____   f. freeze

UNIT
3 **Caring for Your Clothes**

NAME _____

DATE _____

WHAT IS IT?

A. Read the clues. Then unscramble the **boldface** words from the unit that complete the sentences.

1. **CHETNYSITS** _____ are clothes made of manmade, rather than natural, fibers

2. **TRENDTEGE** _____ is the cleaning product used to launder clothes.

3. A **NETMARG** _____ is an item of clothing such as a coat, skirt, or shirt.

4. **SINATS** _____ can become permanent if they're exposed to heat.

5. Use a **MEATS NOIR** _____ _____ to press wrinkles out of your clothing.

6. A **RACE LEBLA** _____ _____ lists washing or dry-cleaning instructions.

7. **NEDOWO RANGESH** _____ _____ keep clothes from bunching up in your closet.

8. Use **HACLEB** _____ to whiten your laundry.

B. Answer the questions with words from the unit.

1. What kind of bleach might ruin colored clothing? _____

2. What water temperature should be used to launder woolen clothing? _____

3. Clothes made of what kind of fabric stretch out when hung on hangers? _____

4. What kind of storage bags can make some types of materials dry out and break down? _____

5. What can you use in your closet to keep your clothes smelling fresh? _____

NAME _____

DATE _____

RECALLING DETAILS

A. Circle a letter to show how each sentence should be completed.

1. You can safely hang a heavy picture on

    a. a nail in a stud.

    b. a molly bolt.

    c. either a. or b.

2. Following a cleaning schedule ensures that

    a. your house doesn't get too dirty.

    b. you remember to do every task.

    c. both a. and b.

3. A good carpet spot cleaner can

    a. repair worn areas.

    b. eliminate vacuuming.

    c. remove pet stains.

4. A kitchen floor needs to be washed

    a. monthly.

    b. weekly.

    c. daily.

5. Houseplants need to be repotted when

    a. the old pots are dirty.

    b. they need more water.

    c. their roots need more room.

6. To mist your houseplants, you'll need a

    a. garden hose.

    b. spray bottle.

    c. watering can.

B. Write **T** or **F** next to each statement to tell whether it is *true* or *false*.

1. _____ On a very bad stain, use twice the recommended amount of spot cleaner.

2. _____ Your kitchen counters and sink should be cleaned daily.

3. _____ All houseplants need plenty of sunlight and water.

4. _____ Before peeling off damaged wallpaper, you must soak the paper thoroughly.

5. _____ Wallpaper adhesive should be applied in a thick layer.

6. _____ By rotating tasks, roommates ensure that they are sharing the housework equally.

NAME _____

DATE _____

COMPREHENSION

A. Write **T** or **F** to show whether each statement is *true* or *false*.

1. _____ You'll save money if you buy food products with well-known brand names.

2. _____ It's best to wash woolen clothing in very hot water.

3. _____ It's all right to hang a sweater on a clothes hanger as long as you fold it later.

4. _____ A microwave oven can shorten the time it takes to prepare dinner.

5. _____ You don't need to find a stud to hang a lightweight picture.

6. _____ All caps and gloves sold in the United States are required to have care labels.

7. _____ Wallpaper adhesive should always be applied thinly.

B. List the words in the box under the correct headings. Then unscramble the last word in each category.

washer	yogurt	cube	synthetics	parboil
blends	cheese	milk	crockpot	simmer
cotton	grate	bake	vacuum	mince

Kinds of Fabric	Cooking Methods	Dairy Products	Home Appliances
_____	_____	_____	_____
_____	_____	_____	_____
_____	_____	_____	_____
_____	_____	_____	_____
OLOW:	RITS-RYF:	CIE MAERC:	RETSOAT:
_____	_____	_____	_____

NAME _____

DATE _____

DICTIONARY DRILL

Many words have *multiple meanings*. That means that the same word can have an entirely different meaning when it's used in a different context. Get out your dictionary. Then, write the definition of each **boldface** word as it was used in this book. Finally, write an entirely different definition for each of the same words.

1. **produce** _____

_____

produce _____

_____

2. **poach** _____

_____

poach _____

_____

3. **dice** _____

_____

dice _____

_____

4. **staple** _____

_____

staple _____

_____

5. **bureau** _____

_____

bureau _____

_____

NAME _____

DATE _____

KEY WORDS IN CONTEXT

A. Circle the hidden words. They may go up, down, across, backward, or diagonally. Check off each word as you find it.

___ **CALORIES**	___ **FLOSS**
___ **UTENSILS**	___ **GREASE**
___ **DANDRUFF**	___ **GERMS**
___ **NUTRIENT**	___ **AEROBIC**
___ **ENDORPHINS**	___ **CALCIUM**
___ **INGREDIENT**	___ **OXYGEN**

```
L K T N E I D E R G N I
S E I R O L A C M B S U
C A L C I U M P L S O T
D F Z R T Y L P N S N E
C A D G H I J I H E G N
I G N A S E H D I N F S
B E X D W P N R O E S I
O R C Q R F T H J G D L
R M V O M U R S D Y E S
E S D E N W F N M X L H
A N B W B S E F L O S S
E S A E R G H D I P A O
```

B. Complete the sentences with words from the puzzle.

1. While doing the same exercise, small people burn fewer _____ than larger people.

2. If your scalp is very dry and flaky, you may need to use a special anti-_____ shampoo.

3. _____ exercise improves your body's ability to utilize _____.

4. Carefully wash _____ such as mixing spoons and spatulas to keep them free of _____.

5. Using dental _____ regularly helps to keep your teeth and gums healthy.

6. Baking soda will put out a _____ fire on the stove.

7. _____ is the mineral that builds strong teeth and bones.

8. _____ are natural chemicals in the brain that relieve stress.

SYNONYMS AND ANTONYMS

A. You know that *synonyms* are words that have the same or almost the same meaning. Find a synonym in the box for each **boldface** word from the book. Write the synonym on the line.

heartbeat	remove	payments	emotions	cleaning
subscribe	injury	counselor	regular	tension

1. **prophylaxis:**

   _____

2. **pulse:**

   _____

3. **feelings:**

   _____

4. **therapist:**

   _____

5. **stress:**

   _____

6. **premiums:**

   _____

7. **extract:**

   _____

8. **damage:**

   _____

9. **routine:**

   _____

10. **enroll:**

   _____

B. *Antonyms* are words that have opposite meanings. Draw a line to connect each **boldface** word from the unit with its antonym.

1. **confide**   a. mild

2. **individual**   b. unusual

3. **specialist**   c. withhold

4. **severe**   d. minor

5. **major**   e. general practitioner

6. **typical**   f. group

NAME _____

DATE _____

WHAT IS IT?

A. Unscramble the vocabulary words that describe each situation.

1. Every April, your nose runs and your eyes itch.

   LAGERLY _____

2. You apply ice to a slightly burned finger.

   TRIFS DIA _____

3. You have stomach cramps and loose bowel movements.

   HEADRAIR _____

4. two pills every six hours

   GESODA _____

5. Your head seems to be spinning and you're afraid you'll fall down.

   SENZISIZD _____

6. You break out in a rash after taking new medicine.

   DISE TEFCEF _____

7. loss of appetite, continual sadness, lack of enjoyment

   NOISESPRED _____

8. uncontrollable vomiting or bleeding

   CYGERMNEE _____

B. Circle the word that correctly completes each sentence.

1. (General / Generic) drugs are usually less expensive than name-brand drugs that are widely advertised.

2. Don't worry about (moles / molds) unless they change size or color.

3. A (tablet / capsule) is a small, flat, hard cake of medicine.

4. A (scrape / bruise) is an injury that discolors the skin without breaking it.

5. Iodine and hydrogen peroxide are examples of commonly used (antiseptics / antibiotics).

CAUSE AND EFFECT

A. Write a letter to match each *cause* on the left with a likely *effect* on the right.

1. _____ drinking and driving   a. hepatitis, AIDS

2. _____ not smoking   b. lung and heart damage

3. _____ peer pressure   c. car accidents

4. _____ bacteria and viruses   d. arrest and conviction

5. _____ using illegal drugs   e. fewer coughs and colds

6. _____ smoking   f. infection

7. _____ regular drug use   g. betraying your own values

8. _____ dirty needle   h. addiction

B. Complete each sentence below with an appropriate *cause* or *effect*.

1. Loss of your parents' trust could be an *effect* of _____

   _____ .

2. Improvement in your sense of taste might be one *effect* of

   _____ .

3. _____ and _____ is the No. 1

   cause of auto accidents.

4. One of every five Americans will die of diseases *caused* by

   _____ .

5. Sexual intercourse with an infected person can *cause* _____ , or

   _____ _____ _____ .

COMPREHENSION

A. Write **F** for *fact* or **O** for *opinion*.

1. _____ Running is a better fitness exercise than walking.

2. _____ Most teenagers have at least occasional problems with acne.

3. _____ Rice and cooked cereal are examples of complex carbohydrates.

4. _____ A good doctor should always question you about your mental health.

5. _____ If you've been sick for only a week, it's best to avoid taking antibiotics.

6. _____ You may wait a long time to be seen in a busy emergency room.

B. Cross off the item that does *not* belong in each group.

1. **information on a prescription label**

   expiration date   dosage   price   special warnings

2. **over-the-counter medicines**

   iodine   antihistamines   penicillin   antacids

3. **infectious diseases**

   alcoholism   colds   hepatitis   mononucleosis

4. **low-fat foods**

   banana   celery   cheese   turkey

5. **unhealthy habits**

   weightlifting   smoking   drinking   taking drugs

NAME _____

DATE _____

DICTIONARY DRILL

A. Complete the crossword puzzle with the *adjective* form of each **boldface** noun. Check a dictionary if you need help.

ACROSS

3. **technology**
   A technician solves ___ problems.

5. **infection**
   Mono is an ___ disease.

6. **medicine**
   If you break a leg, you need ___ help.

7. **sugar**
   Brush your teeth after eating ___ foods.

1: N
2: A
3: T
4: H
5: I
6: M
7: S

DOWN

1. **nutrition**
   Vegetables are ___ foods.

2. **allergy**
   Jake is ___ to peanuts.

4. **hygiene**
   Frequent hand washing is a ___ practice.

B. Circle the correct spelling of each word. Check a dictionary if you're not sure. Then, use each word in a sentence of your own.

antehistamine, antihistamine

vegtable, vegetable

deductible, deductable

hepetitus, hepatitis

antiseptic, antisceptic

temperature, temperture

1. _____

2. _____

3. _____

4. _____

5. _____

6. _____

UNIT 1 — Controlling Your Spending

NAME _____

DATE _____

KEY WORDS IN CONTEXT

A. Circle the hidden words. They may go up, down, across, backward, or diagonally. Check off each word as you find it.

___ **OVERCHARGED** ___ **RECORD**

___ **TEMPTATION** ___ **IMPULSE**

___ **FINANCIAL** ___ **UPDATE**

___ **DOCUMENT** ___ **FRUGAL**

___ **STATEMENT** ___ **MINIMUM**

___ **REGISTER** ___ **FINES**

E	T	A	D	P	U	A	D	R	F	E
S	L	E	K	M	F	I	N	E	S	D
T	J	G	M	H	M	E	S	A	E	Z
A	O	S	E	P	F	R	U	G	A	L
T	H	O	U	E	T	S	R	M	I	A
E	A	L	W	P	O	A	N	U	B	I
M	S	L	J	F	H	U	T	M	E	C
E	W	H	G	C	D	P	A	I	S	N
N	X	A	R	Y	B	N	C	N	O	A
T	N	E	M	U	C	O	D	I	E	N
X	V	D	R	O	C	E	R	M	D	I
O	R	E	G	I	S	T	E	R	Z	F

B. Complete the sentences with words from the puzzle.

1. The _____ to buy things you don't need can sometimes be hard to resist.

2. You will waste money if you don't develop _____ habits.

3. Every month, the bank sends you a _____ listing all your account activities.

4. You must _____ your checkbook _____ every time you make a deposit or withdrawal.

5. A deposit receipt is one kind of _____ _____.

6. Peer pressure can cause you to buy something "on _____."

7. Check sales receipts to make sure you're not being _____.

UNIT
2 — **Banking Basics**

NAME _____

DATE _____

SYNONYMS AND ANTONYMS

A. Complete the crossword puzzle with words from the unit. Answer words are *synonyms* (words with the same or almost the same meanings) of the clue words.

ACROSS

1. money

2. yearly

4. outgo

DOWN

1. penalties

2. sum

3. service charges

B. Remember that *antonyms* are words with opposite meanings. First, unscramble the **boldface** words from the unit. Then, write a letter to match each unscrambled word with its antonym.

1. _____ **AIDVO** _____

2. _____ **LUMTILYP** _____

3. _____ **TIDPOSE** _____

4. _____ **FEDIX** _____

5. _____ **DAD** _____

6. _____ **GASNIV** _____

a. subtract

b. variable

c. spending

d. divide

e. withdrawal

f. attract

WHAT IS IT?

A. Add vowels *(a, e, i, o, u)* to complete the answer words.

1. The letters *APR* stand for

   __NN__ __L P__RC__NT__G__

   R__T__.

2. An __NST__LLM__NT is one
   kind of regular weekly or
   monthly payment.

3. Some debts can also be considered
   to be __NV__STM__NTS.

4. A GR__C__ P__R__ __D is
   an extension of a due date.

5. The amount of money you
   borrow is called the loan
   PR__NC__P__L.

6. You must fill out an
   __PPL__C__T__ __N
   before getting a loan.

7. If a store sells your layaway
   item, ask for a R__F__ND.

8. Banks usually offer the
   lowest L__ __N rates.

B. Circle the word that correctly completes each sentence.

1. You can use a credit card to make purchases over the telephone or
   the (Investment / Internet).

2. The amount of interest you pay on a credit card bill is called a
   (late fee / finance charge).

3. In order to qualify for a loan, the (borrower / lender) must have
   a good credit rating.

4. If you buy something on a (layaway / rent-to-own) plan, you can
   take it home with you.

5. If you're not able to repay a loan, your (co-signer / reference) must
   pay it for you.

6. Some credit (records / cards) are much less expensive than others.

NAME _____

DATE _____

IDENTIFYING MAIN IDEAS

A. Write **T** or **F** to show whether each statement is *true* or *false*.

1. _____ To handle an unexpected expense, you can adjust your budget.

2. _____ Fixed expenses are easier to cut than variable expenses.

3. _____ People who have high incomes don't need to budget.

4. _____ Receipts are important financial records.

5. _____ Your savings earn interest, and your debts cost interest.

6. _____ Going into debt for any reason is always a big mistake.

7. _____ A regular savings contribution—no matter how little—is an important investment.

8. _____ Collateral is something of value that's used to guarantee repayment of a loan.

B. Circle a letter to show how each sentence should be completed.

1. **The two main parts of a budget are**

   a. banks and credit unions.
   b. earnings and expenses.
   c. receipts and credit slips.

2. **The faster you pay off a loan,**

   a. the less money you can save.
   b. the faster your checks bounce.
   c. the less interest you will pay.

3. **On an installment plan, you will pay**

   a. a little at a time.
   b. the least possible interest.
   c. less for a warranty.

NAME _____

DATE _____

COMPREHENSION

1. Explain the different purposes of a *deposit slip* and a *withdrawal slip*.

   _____

   _____

2. Write examples of one *necessary expense* and one *unnecessary expense*.

   _____

   _____

3. What is the common term used for an *overdraft*? _____

4. Name two ways a bad *credit rating* can cause you trouble.

   _____

   _____

5. Why does the *unpaid balance* on your credit card continue to grow even if you don't make more purchases? _____

6. What is a "*balloon payment*"? _____

   _____

7. Name one *variable expense* and one *fixed expense*.

   _____

   _____

8. Name two ways you can be financially prepared for an *emergency*.

   _____

   _____

NAME _____

DATE _____

DICTIONARY DRILL

Notice the **boldface** words from the book. Use a dictionary to look up the other form of the word. Then, write a sentence, using the alternate form. The first one has been done for you.

1. **adjust** (verb)　　　　(noun) _____ *adjustment* _____

   Rudy made an adjustment in his budget this month.

2. **afford** (verb)　　　　(adjective) _____

   _____

3. **excessive** (adjective)　　　　(verb) _____

   _____

4. **payment** (noun)　　　　(verb) _____

   _____

5. **accomplish** (verb)　　　　(noun) _____

   _____

6. **manage** (verb)　　　　(noun) _____

   _____

7. **expense** (noun)　　　　(adjective) _____

   _____

8. **transaction** (noun)　　　　(verb) _____

   _____

9. **risk** (noun)　　　　(adjective) _____

   _____

NAME _____

DATE _____

KEY WORDS IN CONTEXT

A. Circle the hidden words. They may go up, down, across, backward, or diagonally. Check off each word as you find it.

___ CONSIGNMENT	___ DONATED
___ COMPARATIVES	___ BAZAAR
___ OVERSTATE	___ OUTLET
___ CONSUMER	___ BRAND
___ DISCOUNT	___ ESTATE
___ FIXTURES	___ FLAW

```
W E O T R A A Z A B O S
F G V S F D O N A T E D
D Z E U B I H G L V E P
P B R A N D X D I F T C
R S S R T Y O T M O A X
E L T V B N A C U E T D
M S A Q W R E T F R S G
U J T E A F L A W Y E L
S D E P B E N E D C Y S
N C M P T N U O C S I D
O O T R F D W A U A M O
C O N S I G N M E N T P
```

B. Use a puzzle word to correctly complete each sentence.

1. Warehouse stores and _____ chains usually offer the lowest prices on new merchandise.

2. Often used in advertising, _____ are words that end in *-er*, such as *cleaner* and *smoother*.

3. Do you always buy the same _____ of toothpaste?

4. Most ad copy tends to _____ a product's features and benefits.

5. A _____ is a sale of _____ goods to benefit a hospital or a church.

6. You may find a slight _____ in a sweater bought at a factory _____ store.

7. Bathroom _____ include a sink and a bathtub.

8. When Grandpa died, his furniture was sold at an _____ sale.

NAME _____

DATE _____

SYNONYMS AND ANTONYMS

A. Complete the crossword puzzle with words from the unit. Clue words are *synonyms* (words with the same or almost the same meaning) of the answer words.

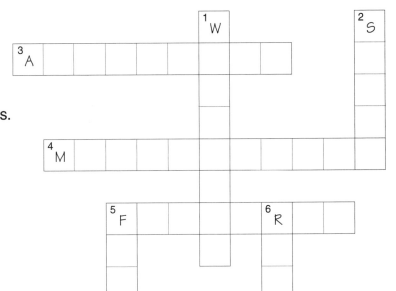

ACROSS

3. helper

4. goods

5. characteristics

7. rule

DOWN

1. guarantee

2. fashion

5. material

6. mend

B. First, unscramble the **boldface** words from the unit. Then, write a letter to match each unscrambled word with its *antonym* (word that means the opposite).

1. _____ a **TENMANREP** _____ stain

2. _____ to **DIVAO** _____ delay

3. _____ **RESIVAR** _____ promptly

4. _____ **EVICTFEED** _____ merchandise

5. _____ **SEDU** _____ furniture

6. _____ **PEACH** _____ prices

a. expensive   c. new   e. departs

b. temporary   d. attract   f. perfect

NAME _____

DATE _____

WHAT IS IT?

A. Unscramble the words that match each definition.

1. a company's "good name,"
   based on honesty and
   performance record:

   TAITPRUNEO _____

2. the approximate price
   of a repair job:

   TEAMITES _____

3. expert repairer of car engines,
   transmissions, etc.:

   CEMCHAIN _____

4. names of people who can
   recommend you as a
   trustworthy person:

   SCENREFEER _____

5. regular payments made
   for insurance coverage:

   SMIRPMUE _____

6. Use this when you work
   with power tools:

   ONUTAIC _____

B. Unscramble the words to complete the sentences.

1. To be safe, read every word on a GINNRAW _____ label.

2. Many professionals ATEENURAG _____ that you will be
   100 percent satisfied with their work.

3. Your YPOILC _____ states all the terms of your insurance
   coverage.

4. If a new product is still under RYAWTRAN _____, there
   will be no charge for repairs.

5. A contractor's SNICELE _____ proves that a repair company
   has experience.

6. Parts and ROBLA _____ are the two main charges on any
   job estimate.

7. If you die, your ICYFAIRNEEB _____ will receive the face
   value of your life insurance policy.

UNIT
(4) **Consumer Rights**

NAME _____

DATE _____

TRUE OR FALSE?

Write **T** or **F** to show whether each statement is *true* or *false*.

1. _____ Write a letter of complaint immediately if you lose your credit card.

2. _____ Buying insurance makes sense if you have several credit cards.

3. _____ Most rebates lower your balance by only a few cents.

4. _____ As a last resort, you can take a disputed claim to Small Claims Court.

5. _____ The Better Business Bureau is a consumer protection organization.

6. _____ An implied warranty is always written in technical language.

7. _____ A warranty does not apply until you've made a good effort to repair the product yourself.

8. _____ Some extended warranties are actually a waste of money.

9. _____ Telemarketers are salespeople who try to sell you telephones.

10. _____ It's risky to do business with a company that has only a post office box number.

11. _____ Your Social Security and driver's license numbers are considered personal information.

12. _____ Until a settlement is made, you don't have to pay a disputed charge on your credit card bill.

NAME _____

DATE _____

COMPREHENSION

Circle a letter to complete the sentence or answer the question.

1. **Service is usually excellent at a**

   a. factory outlet.

   b. church bazaar.

   c. specialty store.

   d. discount store.

2. **In a newspaper classified ad, the abbreviation *obo* means**

   a. or best offer.

   b. often breaks open.

   c. only bargains offered.

   d. other buys optional.

3. **If you see an attractive item marked "as is," you should**

   a. look it over carefully.

   b. ask if it's free.

   c. ask for your money back.

   d. buy it immediately.

4. **How might you save money on repair bills?**

   a. charge them on a credit card

   b. use rebuilt parts instead of new ones

   c. refuse to sign the authorization

   d. put off the repair job for a while

5. **To return an item to the store for cash or credit, you will need to bring**

   a. your receipt.

   b. the product packaging.

   c. proof that it doesn't fit.

   d. both a. and b.

6. **Why is it best to buy a new mattress rather than a used one?**

   a. The cover may be old and worn.

   b. It's less expensive.

   c. The padding may be flattened.

   d. for health reasons

DICTIONARY DRILL

Circle two spelling errors in each sentence. Rewrite the sentences correctly on the writing lines. Check the dictionary if you're not sure of a word's spelling.

1. Comparing differnt brands is an important principal of smart shopping.

   _____

   _____

2. Is this paticular watch water resistent?

   _____

   _____

3. Is it your oppinion that most ads exxagerate?

   _____

   _____

4. Be sure to compare the lables on simalar products.

   _____

   _____

5. It's hard to exchange merchandice if you don't have a reciept.

   _____

   _____

6. Can you interpet all the language on the product warrenty?

   _____

   _____

7. You'll find proffesional servises listed in the yellow pages.

   _____

   _____

8. I wouldn't reccomend a repair service that doesn't garantee its work.

   _____

   _____

NAME _____

DATE _____

KEY WORDS IN CONTEXT

A. Circle the hidden words. They may go up, down, across, backward, or diagonally. Check off each word as you find it.

___ TRAINING	___ BENEFIT
___ CLERICAL	___ CURRENT
___ ADVANCE	___ CHEF
___ PENSION	___ GOAL
___ APPRENTICE	___ TRADE
___ OPPORTUNITY	___ ACADEMY

```
S  Y  T  I  N  U  T  R  O  P  P  O
D  F  A  L  K  G  H  T  E  R  W  A
X  E  S  P  Q  B  R  Y  U  F  B  C
A  H  B  C  P  A  E  L  M  J  G  U
W  C  K  L  I  R  A  N  F  E  O  R
P  U  A  N  K  C  E  W  E  A  S  R
I  O  I  D  I  Y  Z  N  L  F  O  E
G  N  T  R  E  T  O  K  T  M  I  N
G  Y  E  P  O  M  E  S  R  I  A  T
J  L  S  D  B  U  Y  G  A  F  C  D
C  A  V  E  C  N  A  V  D  A  L  E
P  E  N  S  I  O  N  S  E  O  P  Y
```

B. Use puzzle words to correctly complete the sentences.

1. Our department secretary does _____ work.

2. Health insurance is probably the most important job _____.

3. Paula's _____ is to attend the police _____.

4. Luis is now an _____ _____ at a fine downtown restaurant.

5. Grandma Brown now receives a _____, after many years of work for the telephone company.

6. Before you visit the company, check in _____ to see if there are _____ job openings.

7. Roger plans to learn plumbing, his father's _____.

8. On-the-job _____ gives you the _____ to earn while you learn.

NAME _____

DATE _____

SYNONYMS AND ANTONYMS

A. Complete the crossword puzzle. The **boldface** clue words are *synonyms* (words with the same meaning) of the answer words from Unit 2.

ACROSS

4. complete the **coursework**

5. a **portion** of an amount

7. added a new **client**

8. the **language** of the contract

DOWN

1. the **skills** required

2. can **rely** on an employee

3. **maybe** will occur

6. a **regular** income

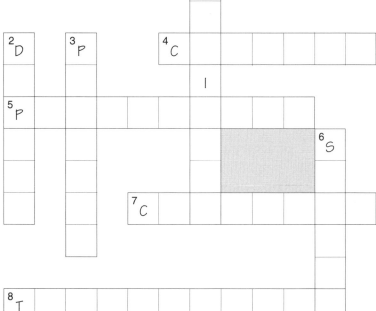

B. Draw a line to match each **boldface** word from Unit 2 with its *antonym* (word with the opposite meaning).

1. **pursue**   a. sell

2. **basic**   b. fire

3. **hire**   c. advanced

4. **purchase**   d. escape

C. Circle the word that correctly completes each sentence.

1. Equivalent qualifications are (equal / unequal).

2. A (teacher / student) at a community college can graduate in two years.

3. A high school diploma or a G.E.D. certificate is (a necessary / an optional) requirement for most jobs.

4. (Reluctant / Eager) workers usually volunteer to help with special projects.

UNIT 3 — Applying for a Job

WHAT IS IT?

A. Unscramble the word from Unit 3 that completes each sentence.

1. SAICGENE _____
   are businesses that represent their
   clients.

2. VERBASTIOBAIN _____
   are short forms of words often used
   in classified ads.

3. An TAPCOLINAIP _____
   is the form you fill out when you
   want a job.

4. NALAMU ROBAL _____
   _____ is work such as
   digging ditches or picking fruit.

5. TENMOSDUC _____
   are important papers such as
   contracts and licenses.

6. STRUPMOCE _____
   are made available to all in
   public libraries.

B. First, unscramble the words. Then, match each unscrambled word with its clue.

1. _____ NATIRGIN _____

2. _____ DOTSCUNIA _____

3. _____ DIRELUGAF _____

4. _____ ROMANDEMISE _____

5. _____ TULIM-KAST _____

6. _____ NOSIMPERIS _____

7. _____ RENTNITE _____

a. saves people from drowning

b. doing several jobs at once

c. crime such as illegal parking

d. course of job instruction

e. cleans schools and offices

f. links networks around the world

g. allows you to do something

UNIT
4 — The Job Interview

RECALLING DETAILS

Complete the sentences with words from the box. Hint: You will *not* use all the words in the box.

complement	beginning	position	walk	curious
documents	reference	notice	calm	record
conclusion	response	complain	talk	spots

1. Try not to _____ too fast when you're leaving a voicemail message.

2. An interviewer will _____ if your hair and fingernails are dirty.

3. It's smart to keep a _____ of all the cover letters you send out.

4. Your _____ to a job ad is your answer.

5. Before an interview, check your clothing for _____ or tears.

6. _____ job applicants appear to be self-confident and capable.

7. The colors orange and red don't _____ each other.

8. The name of a former boss makes a good job _____.

9. It's okay to ask about the salary at the _____ of a job interview.

10. The _____ you're applying for is the job you hope to get.

11. Your birth certificate and driver's license are important _____.

NAME _____

DATE _____

COMPREHENSION

Circle a letter to answer each question.

1. What should you do if you make a mistake on a job application?

   a. Cross it out and write over it.

   b. Apologize to the interviewer.

   c. Get a fresh application and begin again.

   d. Go home and come back tomorrow.

2. What should you wear to a job interview?

   a. only brand new clothes

   b. clean, well-pressed clothes

   c. plenty of cologne.

   d. a formal suit, if you have one

3. You've just written a response to a job ad. What should you do before you mail it?

   a. Check for spelling errors.

   b. Make sure it is neat and clean.

   c. Photocopy it.

   d. a, b, and c

4. Which body signal most impresses a future employer?

   a. slumped shoulders

   b. trembling and perspiring

   c. head hanging low

   d. smiling and standing tall

5. What should you say if an interviewer asks what you can contribute to the company?

   a. "Let me tell you later."

   b. "Hard work and a can-do attitude."

   c. "A large cash investment."

   d. "Good company and a lot of laughs."

6. On a thank-you note for a job interview, how should you sign you name?

   a. with your first name only

   b. in bright red ink

   c. with your new job title

   d. with your first and last names

UNITS
1-4 **JOB SEARCH**

DICTIONARY DRILL

A. Words change form when their part of speech changes. The verb *help*, for example, becomes *helpful* when it changes form to be used as an adjective. Use a dictionary if you need help to complete the charts below.

VERB	NOUN	VERB	ADJECTIVE
1. pronounce	_____	9. impress	_____
2. fail	_____	10. employ	_____
3. communicate	_____	11. write	_____
4. think	_____	12. conclude	_____
5. select	_____	13. consider	_____
6. choose	_____	14. inform	_____
7. clean	_____	15. thank	_____
8. inform	_____	16. question	_____

B. Write an original sentence using . . .

1. the **noun** form of *clean*: _____

_____

2. the **adjective** form of *impress*: _____

_____

3. the **noun** form of *pronounce*: _____

_____

C. Write the correctly spelled word to complete each phrase.

1. _____ *colors*   complimentary   complementary

2. _____ *service*   limousine   limosine

KEY WORDS IN CONTEXT

A. Circle the hidden words. They may go up, down, across, backward, or diagonally. Check off each word as you find it.

___ PRECAUTION   ___ DRESSY

___ EVALUATIONS   ___ GOSSIP

___ CRITICISM   ___ DUES

___ WITHHELD   ___ IMAGE

___ APPROPRIATE   ___ CONTACT

___ IMPRESSION   ___ PAYROLL

S	E	T	A	I	R	P	O	R	P	P	A
X	T	D	R	E	S	S	Y	D	L	W	O
P	C	W	C	A	H	N	J	L	N	I	N
E	A	R	T	R	M	O	K	O	B	T	O
U	T	Y	K	L	I	I	I	S	Z	H	I
X	N	C	R	E	W	T	F	D	P	H	S
U	O	Y	T	O	U	A	I	A	O	E	S
D	C	P	E	A	L	U	T	C	W	L	E
L	U	N	C	H	J	L	K	O	I	D	R
A	X	E	L	I	M	A	G	E	N	S	P
S	R	M	S	E	D	V	S	A	I	P	M
P	I	S	S	O	G	E	A	I	C	O	I

B. Use puzzle words to correctly complete the sentences.

1. Job performance reviews are also called employee _____.

2. You can learn a lot from constructive _____.

3. Party clothes are too _____ to wear to the office.

4. Making good eye _____ when you shake hands creates
   a good first _____.

5. Ask the _____ clerk about deductions that are being
   _____ from your paycheck.

6. To be a member of the union, you will have to pay _____.

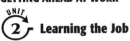
SYNONYMS AND ANTONYMS

A. Complete the crossword puzzle with *synonyms* (words with similar meanings) of the **boldface** clue words. Answers are words you learned in Unit 2.

ACROSS

1. the **goal** of the project

4. **spoken** instructions

6. Everyone doesn't work at the same **rate**.

7. Join the **conversation** at meetings.

DOWN

2. to **teach** yourself

3. a **worker** at a company

4. Employees' contributions should be **appreciated**.

5. to **ask for** clarification

B. Find an *antonym* (word that means the opposite) in the box for each **boldface** word from the unit. Write it on the correct writing line. Hint: You will *not* use all the words in the box.

located	consistently	instructions	frequently	fired
genuine	adequately	clarification	enthusiasm	sincere
positive	promoted	complicated	beforehand	prompt

1. hired / _____

2. confusion / _____

3. simple / _____

4. afterward / _____

5. occasionally / _____

6. rarely / _____

7. negative / _____

8. disinterest / _____

9. false / _____

10. late / _____

NAME _____

DATE _____

WHAT IS IT?

A. Unscramble the word from the unit that matches each clue.

1. steady forward movement
   toward a goal:

   SPROGERS _____

2. extra hours worked beyond
   your regular shift:

   VETROMIE _____

3. time and date reserved
   to do something:

   TOPMINTPANE _____

4. the ability to perform
   a task well:

   MOCPENETEC _____

5. rules or models used
   for comparison:

   DARTSDANS _____

6. the condition of being
   precisely and exactly right:

   CYCARUCA _____

B. Unscramble the words that complete the sentences.

1. The new keyboarder's daily UTOPTU _____ will increase
   as she learns the job.

2. It's really true that CARTCIPE _____ makes CREPEFT
   _____!

3. Speed doesn't count for much if you make too many ROSRER
   _____.

4. "AMERUSE _____ twice, cut CONE _____,"
   said the experienced carpenter.

5. Speed and accuracy are two CHARNEMBSK _____ of success
   on the job.

6. A ENITARE _____ is a worker who is still being taught how
   to do a job.

NAME _____

DATE _____

TRUE OR FALSE?

Write **T** or **F** to show whether each statement is *true* or *false*.

1. _____ A bus schedule is more dependable than many old cars.

2. _____ Workers from different ethnic groups always have trouble working together.

3. _____ You will be fired if your supervisor finds out that you have health problems.

4. _____ If you tend to oversleep, you can't be blamed for being tardy for work.

5. _____ When your work is being criticized, it's best to keep your emotions to yourself.

6. _____ It's never okay to give your work number to family members.

7. _____ Your complaints about your personal life may keep your co-workers from doing their jobs.

8. _____ It's easier to respect other people's traditions once you understand something about them.

9. _____ It's all right to e-mail your friends on the company's computer.

10. _____ Tardiness and absenteeism will usually help you get a good job review.

11. _____ A smart employee will thank her supervisor for constructive criticism.

COMPREHENSION

Circle a letter to complete each statement.

1. **Information about a company's vacation and sick leave benefits**

   a. is stored in a file cabinet.

   b. is not given to new employees.

   c. changes every six months.

   d. can be found in the employee handbook.

2. **The amount of money you get when you cash a paycheck is your**

   a. gross pay.

   b. net pay.

   c. total deduction.

   d. annual salary.

3. **On your first day at work, your employer expects you**

   a. to pay attention and try hard.

   b. to come early and leave late.

   c. to do everything perfectly.

   d. to prove your honesty and integrity.

4. **Federal Income Tax and FICA are payments**

   a. on company loans.

   b. the government makes to you.

   c. added to paychecks.

   d. you make to the government.

5. **Your gross pay, net pay, and all deductions appear on**

   a. the annual report.

   b. company brochures.

   c. the Internet.

   d. your earnings statement.

6. **As a member of a team, it is your responsibility to**

   a. do most of the work yourself.

   b. do things your own way.

   c. cooperate and do your part.

   d. be the team leader.

NAME _____

DATE _____

DICTIONARY DRILL

A. Notice that the clue words are *nouns* from the unit. Complete the crossword puzzle with the *verb* form of each noun. Check a dictionary if you need help.

ACROSS

2. initiative

3. satisfaction

4. employment

5. negotiation

DOWN

1. reliability

3. success

4. entry

B. First, underline two spelling errors in each sentence. (Check a dictionary to make sure you're right!) Then, rewrite the sentence correctly on the writing line.

1. Harrasment is one kind of greivance some employees experience in the workplace.

   _____

   _____

2. A certain amount of gossip ocurrs in all companys.

   _____

   _____

3. Union dews will be deducted from the salery shown on your paycheck.

   _____

   _____

4. If you don't understand the forman's instructions, ask for clarafication.

   _____

   _____

    Saddleback Lifeskills • Saddleback Publishing, Inc. © 2003 • Three Watson, Irvine, CA 92618 • Phone: (888) 735-2225 • Fax: (888) 734-4010 • www.sdlback.com

KEY WORDS IN CONTEXT

A. Circle the hidden words. They may go up, down, across, backward, or diagonally. Check off each word as you find it.

___ **NATIONAL**   ___ **LIBRARY**

___ **RECREATION**   ___ **PUBLIC**

___ **CITIZENS**   ___ **TAX**

___ **CERTIFIED**   ___ **PRIORITY**

___ **MAINTAIN**   ___ **CLINIC**

___ **CONFIRMATION** ___ **SERVICES**

```
C O N F I R M A T I O N
E C R P S E R V I C E S
A L E O N I L K M I B C
S I C R T A X Y R T V Y
D N R X T S T D E I O R
C I E G E I N I P Z L A
I C A H R C F S O E D R
L W T O E C J I G N H B
B Z I G D N O L E S A I
U R O W E S A N B D C L
P Q N I A T N I A M O X
```

B. Complete each sentence with the correct puzzle word.

1. _____ Mail provides the sender with _____ of delivery.

2. _____ parks serve _____ in many ways.

3. _____ Mail is not delivered as quickly as Express Mail.

4. Your _____ dollars are used to develop and _____ public parks.

5. Medicare is a _____ health program for older people.

6. You can get free or low-cost _____ at a public health _____.

7. The Parks and _____ Department is a great source of interesting programs.

UNIT
(2) Emergency Assistance

NAME _____

DATE _____

SYNONYMS AND ANTONYMS

A. You know that *synonyms* are words with the same or nearly the same meaning. Complete the puzzle with synonyms of the clue words. Answers are words from Unit 2.

ACROSS

2. examine

4. walkers

7. lawyer

8. safety

DOWN

1. charges

3. educated

4. maintain

5. gifts

6. aim

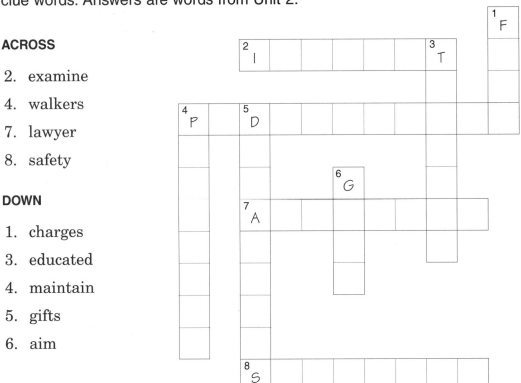

B. *Antonyms* are words with opposite meanings. Write an antonym from the box next to each **boldface** word from the unit.

accidental	shallow	free	include	eventual
discourage	rapidly	rural	guilty	defender

1. **deliberate** / _____

2. **promote** / _____

3. **innocent** / _____

4. **prosecutor** / _____

5. **immediate** / _____

6. **costly** / _____

7. **slowly** / _____

8. **urban** / _____

9. **exclude** / _____

10. **deep** / _____

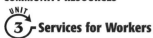
WHAT IS IT?

A. Unscramble the words from Unit 3 to complete the sentences.

1. You should memorize the number on your ISCOLA CRUISETY DARC _____.

2. OSHA stands for ACOUNTCOILAP _____ Safety and Health Administration.

3. You might be able to find a job at the state MEENYLOMPT _____ office.

4. Social Security is funded by your YAPLORL EXSAT _____.

5. You must file a claim to receive unemployment insurance STIFNEEB _____.

6. CEMENTALP _____ offices try to match people with appropriate jobs.

7. The Department of ROBAL _____ is part of the federal government.

8. Worker's POEMTONCSAIN _____ can pay your bills if you are injured.

B. Circle the word that correctly completes each sentence.

1. Proper waste (disposal / proposal) is a safety requirement on the job.

2. Most businesses welcome a visit from an OSHA (inventor / inspector).

3. The Employment Standards Administration is the largest (agency / agent) in the Labor Department.

4. Your state employment office is financed by (federal / state) taxes.

5. Illegal immigrants are not (employed / eligible) for Social Security.

6. You must file (a claim / an application) for a Social Security card.

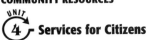

Services for Citizens

RECALLING DETAILS

Circle a letter to correctly complete each sentence.

1. **Life insurance claims may require a**

   a. birth certificate.

   b. death certificate.

   c. voter registration card.

   d. valid driver's license.

2. **To get a copy of your birth certificate, you must be able to tell**

   a. your father's address.

   b. why you want it.

   c. your mother's maiden name.

   d. your current salary.

3. **Instead of casting their ballots at the polls, many voters prefer to**

   a. run for office.

   b. phone in their vote.

   c. vote on the Internet.

   d. vote by mail.

4. **Cities and towns are divided into voting districts called**

   a. polls.

   b. precincts.

   c. political parties.

   d. areas.

5. **The "diversity visa" is also known as a**

   a. Green Card.

   b. deportation.

   c. naturalization.

   d. pink paper.

6. **You must have knowledge of United States history and government to**

   a. register to vote.

   b. get a visa.

   c. become a citizen.

   d. get a marriage certificate.

COMPREHENSION

A. Write **T** for *true* or **F** for *false* next to each statement.

1. _____ "Public resources" and "services for citizens" are the same thing.

2. _____ The FBI is responsible for suicide prevention.

3. _____ If you dial 9-1-1, a police officer will answer the phone.

4. _____ Community shelters protect people from violence.

5. _____ Expert hostage negotiators work for the fire department.

6. _____ Calling a hotline can help you find a date.

7. _____ For every 1,000 U.S. citizens, there are 2.5 law enforcement officers.

8. _____ Firefighters rescue victims of earthquakes and floods.

B. Write a letter to match each *cause* on the left with its *effect* on the right.

1. _____ Eddie files form SS-5.　　　　a. She reregisters to vote.

2. _____ Julie changes her　　　　　　b. He applies for unemployment
political party.　　　　　　　　insurance.

3. _____ Sally gets badly burned　　　c. She files for Worker's
on the job.　　　　　　　　　　Compensation.

4. _____ The company Art works for　　d. He receives a Social Security
goes out of business.　　　　　card.

5. _____ Illegal aliens are caught　　　e. He gets a copy of his
at the border.　　　　　　　　birth certificate.

6. _____ Pete needs to prove his　　　f. They are deported to their
age.　　　　　　　　　　　　native country.

NAME _____

DATE _____

DICTIONARY DRILL

A. The same root word takes different forms, depending on whether it's used as a *verb* or a *noun*. Complete the crossword puzzle with the *verb* form of each clue word. Check a dictionary if you need help.

ACROSS

1. assistance
4. participation
6. enforcement
7. application
8. election

DOWN

2. transportation
3. regulation
5. referral or reference

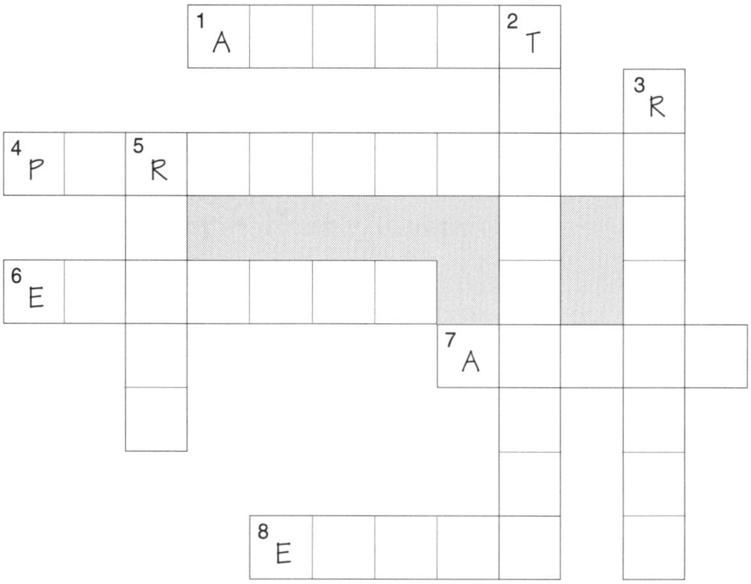

(Crossword grid: 1 Across starts with A; 2 Down starts with T; 3 Down starts with R; 4 Across starts with P; 5 Down starts with R; 6 Across starts with E; 7 Across starts with A; 8 Across starts with E)

B. Words that have entirely different meanings when used in different contexts are called *multiple-meaning words*. First, look in the dictionary to find the **boldface** word in each phrase. Then, write two entirely different meanings for the word.

1. their **interest** lies

   FIRST MEANING: _____

   SECOND MEANING: _____

2. problems are hard to **handle**

   FIRST MEANING: _____

   SECOND MEANING: _____

3. neighborhood **watch** programs

   FIRST MEANING: _____

   SECOND MEANING: _____

4. department **mission** statement

   FIRST MEANING: _____

   SECOND MEANING: _____

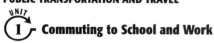
NAME _____

DATE _____

KEY WORDS IN CONTEXT

A. Circle the hidden words. They may go up, down, across, backward, or diagonally. Check off each word as you find it.

___ **ECONOMICAL**   ___ **CARPOOL**

___ **DEFENSIVE**   ___ **BENEFITS**

___ **COMMUTERS**   ___ **TANDEM**

___ **STRENUOUS**   ___ **ROUTE**

___ **HITCHHIKE**   ___ **STROLL**

___ **CYCLISTS**   ___ **STRANGER**

P	B	A	E	V	I	S	N	E	F	E	D
S	V	E	K	I	H	H	C	T	I	H	S
E	R	J	N	S	T	R	O	L	L	X	T
C	H	E	K	E	L	P	E	A	S	I	R
Y	A	O	T	U	F	R	C	V	T	S	E
S	E	R	L	U	P	I	E	B	R	T	N
A	T	D	P	T	M	H	T	G	A	S	U
E	R	A	N	O	W	M	U	S	N	I	O
K	E	Z	N	Q	O	F	O	E	G	L	U
L	S	O	A	D	R	L	R	C	E	C	S
P	C	P	M	B	E	R	D	O	R	Y	A
E	N	S	G	I	L	M	U	P	S	C	E

B. Use a puzzle word to complete each sentence.

1. Some _____ choose to _____ to work instead of driving or taking the bus.

2. Joining a _____ is an _____ way to share the cost of commuting.

3. On a _____ bike, two _____ can ride at the same time.

4. Walking provides many _____, even if your pace isn't _____.

5. When you _____, you entrust your personal safety to a _____.

6. What's the most direct _____ from my house to your house?

7. _____ drivers watch out for obstacles in the road.

UNIT
2 — **Traveling by Bus**

NAME _____

DATE _____

SYNONYMS AND ANTONYMS

A. Use *synonyms* (words with similar meanings) of the **boldface** words to complete the puzzle.

ACROSS

2. car travels on **rails**
5. a **rider**, not a driver
6. **group** of buses
8. gas is **expensive**

DOWN

1. a **driver**, not a rider
3. a bus **timetable**
4. the **charge** for a ride
7. **hints** for reading a bus schedule

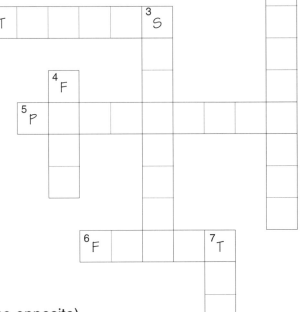

B. Find an *antonym* (word that means the opposite) in the box for each **boldface** word. Use that antonym when you rewrite the sentence correctly. Hint: You will *not* use all the words in the box.

occasional	allows	common	urban	regular
persuades	arrive	subway	walk	hitchhike

1. Buses are the most **unusual** form of mass transit.

   _____

2. Most **rural** transit systems have a fleet of buses.

   _____

3. The schedule shows when you will **depart** at our destination.

   _____

4. An **elevated train** is an underground electric railway.

   _____

5. A bus pass **forbids** a passenger to ride for a month.

   _____

6. The bus driver followed his **random** afternoon route.

   _____

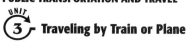
NAME _____

DATE _____

WHAT IS IT?

A. Unscramble the word from Unit 3 that matches each clue.

1. RINETIARY _____:
   written summary of travel plans

4. LONGSA _____:
   catchy saying used in advertising

2. TRUERPADE _____:
   when a train, bus, or plane leaves
   for a destination

5. KRAMAT _____:
   the nation's major rail line for
   passengers

3. TENMOCTRAMP _____:
   private sleeping room on
   a train

6. TORPSAPS _____:
   document necessary for
   foreign travel

B. Use vowels *(a, e, i, o, u)* to complete the words from the unit.

1. You may have to cancel your R__S__RV__T__ __N.

2. Health and safety are important issues for __V__RS__ __S
   travelers.

3. Your C__NF__RM__T__ __N number proves that you made
   a reservation.

4. Discount fares may have some R__STR__CT__ __NS.

5. You can get a passport __PPL__C__T__ __N at the post office.

6. Some countries require __MM__N__Z__T__ __NS before you
   can enter.

7. You may qualify for an exchange or R__F__ND.

8. You must apply for a V__S__ before visiting certain countries.

NAME _____

DATE _____

DRAWING CONCLUSIONS

Circle a letter to answer each question.

1. **What feature would you *not* expect from a 5-star hotel?**

   a. prime location

   b. street parking

   c. elegant lobby

   d. big rooms

2. **What feature would you *not* expect from a 2-star motel?**

   a. coffee in the lobby

   b. air conditioning

   c. clean sheets

   d. workout facilities

3. **What is *not* a benefit of traveling by plane?**

   a. no security checks

   b. discount fares

   c. speedy arrival

   d. time to read

4. **What is *not* a benefit of traveling with a friend?**

   a. sharing expenses

   b. pleasant company

   c. different interests

   d. sharing clothes

5. **Which would *not* be a current travel resource?**

   a. hotel brochure

   b. encyclopedia article

   c. guidebook

   d. TV travel channels

6. **What is *not* a benefit of traveling by automobile?**

   a. Set your own schedule.

   b. auto depreciation

   c. Enjoy the scenery.

   d. unlimited baggage

COMPREHENSION

A. Circle the word that correctly completes each sentence.

1. (Carpooling / Hitchhiking) can have very serious consequences.

2. Mass transit must be (discounted for / accessible to) disabled riders.

3. Walking improves heart and (lung / liver) function.

4. In most states, a bicycle is legally regarded as a (nuisance / vehicle).

5. Some cities have created special (routes / lanes) to speed buses along their way.

6. Walking is the oldest and most basic form of (commuting / transportation).

7. (An index / A legend) explains the symbols on a map.

8. When a regular route is blocked, the bus will have to make a (transfer / detour).

B. Answer the questions in complete sentences.

1. Why do fewer buses run on weekends than on weekdays?

_____

_____

2. Why is it a good idea for regular walkers to vary their routes once in a while?

_____

_____

_____

DICTIONARY DRILL

A. When you change a word's part of speech, you almost always change its form. The verb *locate*, for example, becomes *location* when you change it to a noun. Use a dictionary to help you complete the chart below.

ADJECTIVE	NOUN
1. _____	benefit
2. decent	_____
3. _____	option
4. _____	scenery
5. economical	_____
6. moderate	_____
7. _____	environment
8. enthusiastic	_____
9. _____	distance
10. _____	protection

B. Circle the correctly spelled word in each group. Check a dictionary if you're not sure.

1. hitchiker   hitchhiker   hichhiker

2. accommodations   accomadations   acommadations

3. accesible   accesable   accessible

4. liberries   libraries   librarys

5. passengers   passangers   passingers

6. itinerery   itinarrary   itinerary

7. immunizations   immunazations   immunezations

8. brosure   brochure   broshure

UNIT 1 — Becoming a Good Driver

NAME _____

DATE _____

KEY WORDS IN CONTEXT

A. Circle the hidden words. They may go up, down, across, backward, or diagonally. Check off each word as you find it.

___ **LICENSE**　　___ **PERMIT**

___ **HANDBOOK**　　___ **INDEX**

___ **TRAINING**　　___ **MINOR**

___ **TRAFFIC**　　___ **VALID**

___ **DEFROSTER**　　___ **YIELD**

___ **SUPERVISED**　　___ **GEAR**

```
W  E  T  R  A  F  F  I  C  M  D  S
P  F  D  C  S  X  J  U  K  L  O  U
A  D  S  M  F  G  H  L  E  E  S  P
O  L  E  Y  I  T  R  I  S  W  A  E
Y  P  I  F  B  N  Y  K  V  G  V  R
C  G  E  A  R  I  O  S  C  N  H  V
S  L  K  X  J  O  D  R  E  I  G  I
E  D  H  E  B  U  S  A  O  N  F  S
Q  I  O  D  L  P  B  T  L  I  D  E
Y  L  N  N  E  H  F  D  E  A  S  D
T  A  H  I  G  D  T  I  M  R  E  P
H  V  L  I  C  E  N  S  E  T  L  C
```

B. Use puzzle words to correctly complete the sentences.

1. Check the _____ to find a street's location on a city map.

2. After taking a driver education class, Dexter is ready for driver

   _____.

3. A _____ is someone younger than 18 years old.

4. Turn on your _____ if your windshield is icy.

5. Good drivers _____ the right-of-way when necessary.

6. The driver _____ issued by the state explains the rules of

   the road.

7. Before pulling into _____, Helen always looks over her

   shoulder.

NAME _____

DATE _____

SYNONYMS AND ANTONYMS

A. Find a *synonym* (word that means the same or almost the same) in the box for each **boldface** word from the unit. Write the synonym on the line.

add-ons	preowned	worth	upkeep	guarantee	mandatory
examine	gasoline	label	policy	repairman	recommended

1. **warranty** / _____

2. **mechanic** / _____

3. **suggested** / _____

4. **sticker** / _____

5. **accessories** / _____

6. **inspect** / _____

7. **value** / _____

8. **fuel** / _____

9. **maintenance** / _____

10. **used** / _____

B. You know that *antonyms* are words with opposite meanings. Circle the antonym that correctly completes each sentence below.

1. A new car's sticker price is always (firm / negotiable).

2. Ed needs to (borrow / lend) money to buy a used car.

3. A dealership buys new cars at the (retail / wholesale) rate.

4. More expensive cars have higher (loss / profit) margins.

5. Before deciding to buy a used car, ask your mechanic to do a (thorough / careless) inspection.

6. An (exceptional / average) car is driven about 12,000 miles per year.

7. Optional accessories usually (subtract / add) a lot to the price of a new car.

NAME _____

DATE _____

WHAT IS IT?

A. Write a letter to match each **boldface** word or phrase with its description.

1. _____ **estimate**   a. written proof of purchase

2. _____ **road hazard**   b. the electrical system that starts a car

3. _____ **ignition**   c. percentage of a purchase payable to the state

4. _____ **tire rotation**   d. approximate cost of a repair

5. _____ **receipt**   e. a dangerous condition on a street or highway

6. _____ **sales tax**   f. exchange of tires from front to back

7. _____ **jumper cables**   g. device to start a dead battery from another car's battery

B. Complete the sentences with words from the unit.

1. It's best to change your car's _____ every 3,000 miles.

2. The _____ _____ cleans the air that goes into the cylinders' combustion chambers.

3. Tires will wear out too soon if the _____ _____ is not correct.

4. In frigid weather, a car's _____ loses much of its strength.

5. Turn off your car's _____ when you're connecting jumper cables.

6. Leaving your _____ on when your car is parked will drain your battery.

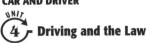
RECALLING DETAILS

Circle a letter to show how each sentence should be concluded.

1. **When a car *depreciates*,**

   a. it loses some of its value.

   b. you no longer appreciate it.

   c. it will be very hard to sell.

2. **A car's *odometer* measures its**

   a. fuel level.

   b. odor level.

   c. mileage.

3. **You pay a charge called the *VLF* when you register a car in California. VLF means**

   a. Value Less Financing.

   b. Variable Lifetime File.

   c. Vehicle License Fee.

4. ***Collision* insurance pays for damages**

   a. that were your own fault.

   b. caused by another driver.

   c. costing less than $1,000.

5. **If you ignore a traffic ticket and fail to appear in court, you can**

   a. lose your car.

   b. lose your license.

   c. pay bail instead.

6. **If you drive while your license is *suspended* or *revoked*, you**

   a. are considered a negligent driver.

   b. will serve time in jail.

   c. must notify the police.

7. **A driver's *alcohol impairment* is measured by his or her BAC. BAC means**

   a. Bad Actor Category.

   b. Blood Alcohol Conviction.

   c. Blood Alcohol Concentration.

COMPREHENSION

A. Categorize the words in the box under the correct headings. Check off each word as you write it on the list.

liability	legend	tailgating	construction
headlights	heater	coverage	compass rose
deductible	index	battery	daydreaming
speeding	fog	collision	playground
drizzle	engine	symbols	recklessness

PARTS OF A CAR

_____

_____

_____

_____

PARTS OF A MAP

_____

_____

_____

_____

ROAD HAZARDS

_____

_____

_____

CAR INSURANCE

_____

_____

_____

Write a heading for the four words that remain in the box.

_____

B. Unscramble the mystery word that matches each clue.

1. RELADE _____ :
   will sell you a car

2. UNLATER _____ :
   like a parking gear

3. PARM _____ :
   leads onto the freeway

4. SINLAGS _____ :
   use these before you turn

5. SNALE _____ :
   don't change them too often

6. DEPLA _____ :
   you step on it

NAME _____

DATE _____

DICTIONARY DRILL

Find each **boldface** word in the dictionary. First, count the syllables (separate sounds in a word) and write the number on the line. Then, write the dictionary definition.

1. **tachometer** _____ syllables

   _____

   _____

   _____

2. **alignment** _____ syllables

   _____

   _____

   _____

3. **parallel** _____ syllables

   _____

   _____

   _____

4. **alternator** _____ syllables

   _____

   _____

   _____

5. **right of way** _____ syllables

   _____

   _____

   _____

6. **cite** _____ syllables

   _____

   _____

   _____

7. **forfeit** _____ syllables

   _____

   _____

   _____